Our Best Friends

Guinea Pigs

Our Best Friends

The Boxer
Caring for Your Mutt
The German Shepherd
The Golden Retriever
The Labrador Retriever
The Poodle
The Shih Tzu
The Yorkshire Terrier

Ferrets
Gerbils
Guinea Pigs
Hamsters
Lizards
Rabbits
Snakes
Turtles

Our Best Friends

Guinea Pigs

Janice Biniok

ELDORADO INK

Produced by OTTN Publishing, Stockton, New Jersey

Eldorado Ink
PO Box 100097
Pittsburgh, PA 15233
www.eldoradoink.com

Printed and bound in Malaysia.

First printing

1 3 5 7 9 8 6 4 2

Library of Congress Cataloging-in-Publication Data

Biniok, Janice.
Guinea pigs / Janice Biniok.
p. cm. — (Our best friends)
ISBN 978-1-932904-29-1 (library edition)
ISBN 978-1-932904-37-6 (trade edition)
1. Guinea pigs as pets—Juvenile literature. I. Title.
SF459.G9B54 2008
636.935'92—dc22

2008033059

Photo credits: Courtesy American Animal Hospital Association, 75; Courtesy The American Rabbit Breeders Association, Inc., 35; © istockphoto.com/Seb Chandler, 28; © istockphoto.com/Christoph Ermel, 81; © istockphoto.com/Alanna Jurden, 19; © istockphoto.com/Kevin Kudrna, 101; © istockphoto.com/pamspix, 88, 90; © istockphoto.com/Olga Solovei, 46; © istockphoto.com/suemack, 98; © istockphoto.com/Eline Spek, 8; © 2008 Jupiterimages Corporation, 3, 25, 32, 37, 41, 50, 68; Library of Congress, 26; © OTTN Publishing, 70; Used under license from Shutterstock, Inc., 10, 11, 12, 14, 15, 17, 20, 23, 24, 27, 29, 31, 38, 42, 43, 44, 47, 49, 51, 53 (both), 55, 56, 57, 59, 61, 62, 66, 69, 71, 74, 77, 78, 79, 82, 85, 86, 89, 92, 93, 95, 96, 99, 102, "Fun Fact" icon, cover (All images front and back).

TABLE OF CONTENTS

	Introduction by Gary Korsgaard, DVM	6
1	Is a Guinea Pig Right for You?	9
2	Guinea Pig History and Breeds	23
3	Finding the Right Guinea Pig	37
4	The Best Possible Beginning	46
5	Nutrition, Exercise, Grooming, and Training	59
6	Health Issues Your Guinea Pig May Face	74
7	Enjoying Your Guinea Pig	88
	Organizations to Contact	104
	Further Reading	106
	Internet Resources	107
	Index	108
	Contributors	112

Introduction

Gary Korsgaard, DVM

The mutually beneficial relationship between humans and animals began long before the dawn of recorded history. Archaeologists believe that humans began to capture and tame wild goats, sheep, and pigs more than 9,000 years ago. These animals were then bred for specific purposes, such as providing humans with a reliable source of food or providing furs and hides that could be used for clothing or the construction of dwellings.

Other animals had been sought for companionship and assistance even earlier. The dog, believed to be the first animal domesticated, began living and working with Stone Age humans in Europe more than 14,000 years ago. Some archaeologists believe that wild dogs and humans were drawn together because both hunted the same prey. By taming and training dogs, humans became more effective hunters. Dogs, meanwhile, enjoyed the social contact with humans and benefited from greater access to food and warm shelter. Dogs soon became beloved pets as well as trusted workers. This can be seen from the many artifacts depicting dogs that have been found at ancient sites in Asia, Europe, North America, and the Middle East.

The earliest domestic cats appeared in the Middle East about 5,000 years ago. Small wild cats were probably first attracted to human settlements because plenty of rodents could be found wherever harvested grain was stored. Cats played a useful role in hunting and killing these pests, and it is likely that grateful humans rewarded them for this assistance. Over time, these small cats gave up some of their aggressive wild behaviors and began living among humans. Cats eventually became so popular in ancient Egypt that they were believed to possess magical powers. Cat statues were placed outside homes to ward off evil spirits, and mummified cats were included in royal tombs to accompany their owners into the afterlife.

Today, few people believe that cats have supernatural powers, but most pet owners feel a magical bond with their pets, whether they are dogs, cats, hamsters, rabbits, horses, or parrots. The lives of pets and their people become inextricably intertwined, providing strong emotional and physical rewards for both humans and animals. People of all ages can benefit from the loving companionship of a pet. Not surprisingly, then, pet ownership is widespread. Recent statistics indicate that about 60 percent of all households in the United States and Canada have at least one pet, while the figure is close to 50 percent of households in the United Kingdom. For millions of people, therefore, pets truly have become their "best friends."

Finding the best animal friend can be a challenge, however. Not only are there many types of domesticated pets, but each has specific needs, characteristics, and personality traits. Even within a category of pets, such as dogs, different breeds will flourish in different surroundings and with different treatment. For example, a German Shepherd may not be the right pet for a person living in a cramped urban apartment; that person might be better off caring for a smaller dog like a Toy Poodle or Shih Tzu, or perhaps a cat. On the other hand, an active person who loves the outdoors may prefer the companionship of a Labrador Retriever to that of a small dog or a passive indoor pet like a goldfish or hamster.

The joys of pet ownership come with certain responsibilities. Bringing a pet into your home and your neighborhood obligates you to care for and train the pet properly. For example, a dog must be housebroken, taught to obey your commands, and trained to behave appropriately when he encounters other people or animals. Owners must also be mindful of their pet's particular nutritional and medical needs.

The purpose of the OUR BEST FRIENDS series is to provide a helpful and comprehensive introduction to pet ownership. Each book contains the basic information a prospective pet owner needs in order to choose the right pet for his or her situation and to care for that pet throughout the pet's lifetime. Training, socialization, proper nutrition, potential medical issues, and the legal responsibilities of pet ownership are thoroughly explained and discussed, and an abundance of expert tips and suggestions are offered. Whether it is a hamster, corn snake, guinea pig, or Labrador Retriever, the books in the OUR BEST FRIENDS series provide everything the reader needs to know about how to have a happy, well-adjusted, and well-behaved pet.

Guinea pigs make great pets, because they are easy to care for—as well as extremely cute!

CHAPTER ONE

Is a Guinea Pig Right for You?

Guinea pigs are delightful little creatures that have been cherished as pets for hundreds of years. It's easy to see why they have remained so popular throughout the ages. Their gemlike eyes and plush fur make them adorable and eminently touchable. They come in such a varied assortment of colors and hair length that there is a Guinea pig to satisfy anyone's desires and tastes. Best of all, they are hardy, clean, and easy to care for, which makes them a very practical choice for a pet.

Whether it is the charmingly cute looks or practicality that attracted you to the Guinea pig, there are even more delights beneath the surface of this amazing animal. Guinea pigs have interesting and very individualistic personalities. They indicate their preferences quite obviously through vocalizations and body language. They can also become very attached to their owners, as evidenced by their show of trust and calmness in their owners' arms.

It would seem that a Guinea pig would make a great pet for just about anyone. Indeed, he's a perfect companion for a great many people, but is he right for you? That depends on how much time you have and whether you can provide the proper care and living conditions to keep a little "piggy" happy.

The Guinea pig is simple to care for, compared to higher-maintenance

The Guinea pig's name may have come from a British tendency to refer to exotic or far-off places as "Guinea"—such as New Guinea, shown on this 19th-century map.

animals like dogs and cats, but they're not quite as easy as fish or some reptiles (although they are a lot more cuddly). On the pet-maintenance scale, Guinea pigs fall somewhere in the middle. Learning what the Guinea pig is and what his needs are will help you decide if you are up to the task of piggy keeping.

MYTHS AND MISNOMERS

First and foremost, it should be noted that the Guinea pig does not come from the Guinea region of West Africa, or from New Guinea, an island just north of Australia. The scientific name for the domestic Guinea pig is *caviidae porcellus*—which is why it is often called a "cavy" for short—a species that originated in the Andes region of South America. So how did this animal come to be named?

There are many theories about the origins of the name "Guinea pig." One theory suggests that *Guinea* is a mispronunciation of Guyana, a South American country where traders may have acquired the animals for export to Europe. Another is that when these animals were first introduced to Europe, they may have been sold for a guinea (a denomination of British currency) apiece. However, English-speakers in the 17th and 18th centuries often used the term "Guinea" to refer to any far-off, unknown country, so the name "Guinea pig" was probably

Although there are several wild members of the cavia genus, the domestic Guinea pig, known scientifically as *caviidae porcellus*, is now extinct in the wild.

coined to refer to the animal's foreign origins.

It is also important to note that the Guinea pig is not really a pig. The only physical characteristics he appears to share with the porcine species are his short legs and stocky build. There are some wild theories as to how this misnomer occurred, including the supposition that Guinea pig meat—the Guinea pig has long been valued as a food source in South America—tastes like pork. More than likely, though, his surname was derived from the noises he makes. A Guinea pig's shrill squeal sounds just like the cry of a pig!

Although Guinea pigs can be surprisingly loud for their size, their most raucous vocalizations are reserved for getting their owners' attention at feeding time or alerting their Guinea pig buddies to potential danger (a very valuable survival trait in the wild). For the most part, they are quiet pets and engage in more subtle vocalizations. The chattering noise of a contented Guinea pig is often called a "purr." Somewhere between the purr and the squeal, the Guinea pig has a range of whistles that he also uses to communicate.

While the Guinea pig's noisemaking is endearing to those who love an interactive, expressive pet, it may not be so highly prized by those who relish quiet. In any case, it is a good idea to keep a Guinea pig housed outside the bedroom.

Guinea pigs make great family pets.

A Guinea pig uses his mouth, tongue, and teeth to find out more about his environment.

PHYSICAL CHARACTERISTICS

Many people are surprised to discover that the Guinea pig is actually a rodent. He is related to the mouse, rat, and porcupine. Maybe it is the lack of a tail (Guinea pigs actually have the vestige of a tail that can be felt at the base of the spine) that makes it confusing to pinpoint just what kind of animal he really is, but the Guinea pig does have a number of very obvious rodent-like characteristics.

THE HEAD: The most distinguishing rodent characteristics of the Guinea pig are found on its head. The Guinea pig's long, sharp incisor teeth are a good example. They serve as an effective weapon, eating utensil, nest-building tool, and grooming implement. These teeth grow continuously to keep up with the wear of constant gnawing. Because of this, Guinea pigs require a never-ending supply of gnawing materials. Their teeth also need to be checked periodically to make sure they don't become overgrown.

A Guinea pig's teeth also serve as a "feeler" to the outside world. A curious Guinea pig will often take a little chomp of something to figure out what it is. He's checking to see if it's soft or hard, if it's something he can gnaw on, or if it's something he can eat. Normally, these are light, little, experimental nips, but you still don't want to get in the habit of sticking your fingers in front of your Guinea pig's mouth and tempting him to nip you. What starts out as a fun little game of nipping may eventually turn into some serious bites.

The Guinea pig's eyes, too, resemble the round, convex eyes of other rodents. His semifloppy ears are hairless, like those of other rodents. And, of course, his nose can quiver just as adorably as a little mouse's. But what makes the Guinea pig stand apart from creatures we might consider vermin is his strong attachment to people.

Although his eyesight is not known to be exceptional, a Guinea pig most definitely shows a spark of recognition when he sees his owner. Those leathery ears possess extraordinary hearing, and he quickly learns to recognize the sound of his owner's voice (or the sound of a refrigerator door). That wonderful aquiline nose seems perfectly designed to fit snuggly in the crook of a human's arm, a place where many Guinea pigs burrow to feel more secure.

BODY: More proof that the Guinea pig was destined to be a companion to people is his oblong body, which is just the right size and shape to fit in a human's arms. Adult Guinea pigs are about eight to ten inches (20 to 25 cm) long and weigh two to three pounds (1 to 1.4 kg)—big enough to cuddle and small enough to carry.

The most distinctive feature of the body is the hair that covers it. This hair comes in such a diverse variety of textures, lengths, and colors that it's hard to believe Guinea

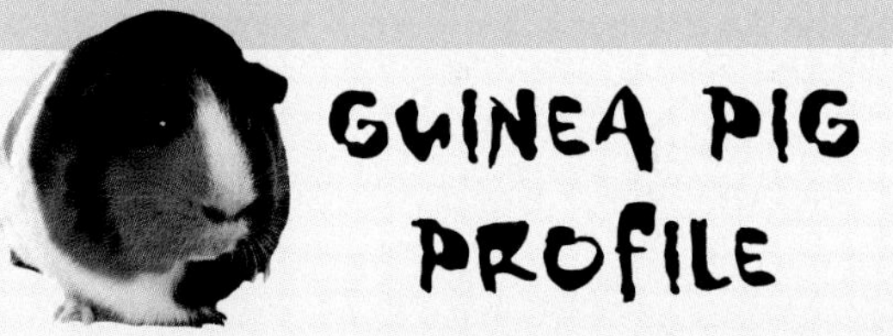

Species: Caviidae porcellus
Size: Up to 10 inches (25 cm) long
Weight: 2–3 lbs. (1–1.4 kg)
Shedding: Low to moderate
Diet: Herbivorous
Activity: Morning and evening
Life span: 5–7 years
Sociability: Herd animal
Gender definitions: Boar (male); sow (female)
Offspring definition: Pups

pigs all belong to the same species. The hair of a Teddy (or Rex) Guinea pig is frizzy. The hair of a Peruvian is long and silky. The hair of a Satin Guinea pig has a distinctive sheen. And the coat of an Abyssinian appears to be cowlicked all over—fanciers call these circular cowlicks "rosettes." There are many other hair variations as well.

Different hair, of course, requires different care. If you like luxurious long hair, be prepared to spend the time required for its upkeep. Guinea pig hair tangles just as easily as human hair. But if you'd rather have a wash-and-wear kind of piggy, there are plenty of smooth-coated, short-haired breeds to choose from.

Legs and Feet: The Guinea pig's sturdy body may make him appear unbreakable, but his legs and feet belie that impression. These delicate appendages are surprisingly small compared to the rest of his physique, and they are likely to be the first to break if you drop your Guinea pig. So handle your piggy with care!

Different Guinea pig breeds have a wide variety of hair lengths and textures. This Peruvian, for example, has hair that is long and silky.

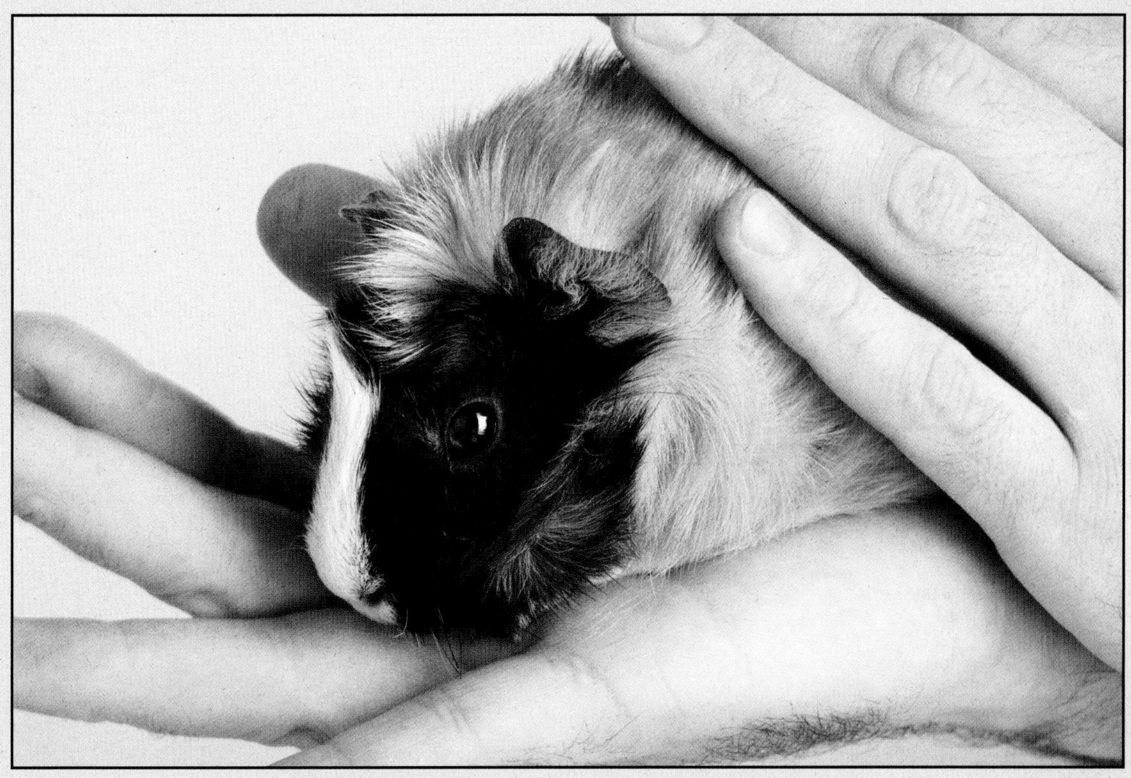

Guinea pigs are nervous creatures, and they require careful handling. This is especially true when they are young. If you handle your Guinea pig properly, and do so often, he will learn to relax and trust you when you want to hold him.

Because the bottoms of a Guinea pig's feet are padded, he should not be kept in a cage with a wire-grate floor, as his feet can become sore. Make sure your Guinea pig has soft footing in his cage. A layer of newspaper underneath some type of cage bedding, such as wood shavings, is ideal.

The pads of the feet provide ample traction for the Guinea pig, as do the sharp little claws on each foot. Guinea pigs are amazingly fast, despite their short legs. There are four toes on each of the Guinea pig's front feet, and three toes on each rear foot. Since the claws grow continuously and rarely get worn down adequately in captivity, it is important to check a Guinea pig's feet regularly and trim his claws as needed.

TEMPERAMENTAL CHARACTERISTICS

Like all animals, the Guinea pig has inherited temperamental traits

FAST FACT

Be prepared to spend at least $250 to get started in Guinea pig keeping, to cover the cost of your pet and his cage, food, and supplies. The costs may be much higher if you opt for a show-quality pig or more luxurious accommodations for your pet.

through the process of natural selection. Just like the evolution of physical characteristics, these temperamental traits have helped the species survive in the wild for thousands of years. Many of these traits remain intact, even though the animals have been domesticated. Your pet Guinea pig will instinctively prefer the company of other Guinea pigs and will flee from threats of danger, even though he is far removed from the wild herds of Guinea pigs in South America.

A CREPUSCULAR CREATURE: One of the traits that give the Guinea pig an advantage as a pet over other rodents is the fact that Guinea pigs are active during the morning and evening. They sleep during midday and at night. While other pet rodent owners must watch their nocturnal pets sleep all day, Guinea pig owners get to watch their pet's amusing antics during breakfast and dinner! Guinea pigs also aren't as inclined to keep their owners up all night with nighttime noisemaking. This is a great advantage for people who want an easy-to-care-for pet they can actually interact with during daylight hours.

HERD ANIMALS: In the wild, Guinea pigs find greater safety living in a group. They can warn each other about approaching danger with their loud squeals. They can take advantage of each other's dens when fleeing predators. This is why many experts recommend getting Guinea pigs in pairs. There are plenty of Guinea pigs that are just as happy to live on their own, provided they receive plenty of handling and attention from their owners, but others become lonely and depressed by themselves.

Since most pet owners can rarely afford the amount of time to keep a lone Guinea pig happy, it may be wiser to consider a pair. Are you

FAST FACT

According to the *Guinness Book of World Records*, the oldest Guinea pig lived 14 years, 10.5 months.

Your Guinea pig will probably appreciate having a friend to play with. Keep in mind, though, that not all Guinea pigs will get along.

prepared for the expenses of housing and maintaining two Guinea pigs? How about more than two? It's not unusual to get carried away with your pig-keeping hobby. As any Guinea pig fancier will tell you, these animals can become highly addictive!

When keeping more than one Guinea pig, be aware that Guinea pigs get along best if they are raised together from a young age. Buying two from the same litter or adopting a bonded pair from a shelter is the easiest way to keep peace in your Guinea pig world. It's usually best to get two of the same sex, unless you want to end up with many, many more than two! If you decide to keep a lone pig, a boar (that is, a male Guinea pig) is likely to be the happiest in that type of situation.

Because Guinea pigs are herd animals, they do have a social order, just like other animals that live in groups. There will be a dominant personality in any group of Guinea pigs, and the other Guinea pigs will respect the dominant pig and leave him alone (even though they may compete with lower-order Guinea pigs for resources such as food or resting places).

Dominance is not usually enforced as strictly in a domestic situation as it is in wild groups of cavies, but it still may result in some nasty fights. Strangely, though, the pigs rarely injure each other severely during these skirmishes. Guinea pigs that exert their authority a little too adamantly may have to be removed from the group.

Prey Animals: The Guinea pig is also a prey animal, which means that, in the wild, it is hunted and eaten by predators. For this reason, the Guinea pig is naturally alert and high-strung. He is always on the lookout for danger. Fast or sudden movements on your part, or a loud noise, are liable to send your Guinea pig diving for cover!

It's normal for a Guinea pig to exhibit some anxiety when you try to pick him up, but a tame Guinea pig will quickly settle down once in your hands. This is why it's so important to handle your Guinea pig frequently, so he can learn to trust you and feel safe with you. Guinea pigs that do not receive much handling can become very skittish around humans (and everything else).

Like many other prey animals, Guinea pigs are herbivores. That is, they eat only vegetation. Guinea pigs enjoy fresh grass (not sprayed with lawn chemicals, of course), but they also have several other favorites. Carrots are a special delicacy, as are some fresh fruits like apples and pears. Providing your Guinea pig with a variety of plant material to eat, in addition to his commercial feed, is required not only to keep your piggy happy—it's also required for his health.

Everyone in the household should spend some time with a Guinea pig before bringing one home, to make sure no one has allergies to this particular species.

GUINEA PIGS AND CHILDREN

Guinea pigs and children go together like ice cream and chocolate cake. However, there are a couple of guidelines to keep in mind. First, an adult should always be the animal's primary caregiver. Children should not be expected to shoulder complete responsibility for a Guinea pig, as efforts to teach a child responsibility in this way will most likely result in the neglect and suffering of a living creature.

Second, parental supervision and guidance are paramount. Some Guinea pig rescue organizations refuse to adopt out Guinea pigs to families who plan to keep the animal in a child's bedroom, because this type of living arrangement is conducive to a lack of parental supervision. A parent should always be present when children are handling or caring for the Guinea pig.

Third, make sure that the interactions you allow between the Guinea pig and children are age-appropriate. Children under the age of five or six are not always aware that their actions can cause pain to other creatures, and they do not have the coordination to handle a Guinea pig safely. But that doesn't mean a younger child cannot enjoy petting a Guinea pig held by an adult. They are also old enough to help with care duties such as feeding, cleaning the cage, and picking fresh grass for your little piggy to savor.

There are all kinds of activities children can enjoy doing with a Guinea pig, including constructing chew toys out of cardboard tubes, tissue boxes, or paper bags. One of the most interesting aspects of having a Guinea pig involves simply observing the animal. By watching,

Young children can be taught how to properly handle, pet, and feed a Guinea pig. However, an adult should always be in the room when a child is holding a Guinea pig.

A Guinea pig may play well with other pets that you have. However, you must always supervise when your piggy is playing with other pets.

your children will learn to recognize his communication signals and discover what he likes and doesn't like.

A Guinea pig can provide a wonderful educational experience for children, but you must always remember that it is a small creature that can be easily injured. Providing adequate supervision, establishing rules of conduct, and learning how to properly handle your Guinea pig yourself will help ensure your Guinea pig's safety.

GUINEA PIGS AND OTHER PETS

When it comes to other pets, the main thing to remember is that Guinea pigs are prey animals. Whether or not they can cohabit with predators like dogs and cats depends a lot on each animal's temperament. Dogs have a natural dislike for rodents, and a dog with a high prey drive, such as a German Shepherd or a Siberian Husky, is likely to kill a Guinea pig in short order. Some dogs do, however, adjust quite well to a Guinea pig's presence. Even if they do not become soul mates, they are capable of learning to tolerate each other.

Cats will rarely target a Guinea pig as prey, as cats prefer rodents of bite-size varieties (think field mice, for example), but again, this depends on the individual cat's personality. When in doubt, it is always safest to bring a Guinea pig home on a trial basis to see how the animals interact. Precautions need to be taken to make sure the Guinea pig is kept safely out of a predator's reach.

As prey animals, Guinea pigs are naturally nervous. Even if your dog or cat doesn't seem to pay your Guinea pig any mind, it might become obvious that your piggy is stressed by the threat of predators so close to his living quarters. If this is the case, it is kindest to find your Guinea pig a new home where he will feel more at ease.

Many Guinea pigs are kept in the company of rabbits and even develop close bonds with them. Since both are prey animals, and both have similar tastes in food, rabbits and Guinea pigs have a lot in common. Even so, Guinea pigs are much smaller than most rabbits, so Guinea pig–rabbit interactions should be supervised. Each should have its own living accommodations and be fed separately to avoid squabbles.

THE BEST ENVIRONMENT FOR A GUINEA PIG

The best environment for a Guinea pig is created when the animal is treated like a cherished house pet. If his cage is kept in a frequently used room, where family members can see him and interact with him regularly, he will seem like a member of the family. He will even learn to recognize and respond to his favorite people!

Occasionally, Guinea pigs are kept as outdoor pets in hutches, but this type of living arrangement often gives a Guinea pig very little human contact. This kind of "out of sight, out of mind" situation can also leave a Guinea pig prone to neglect. If you are interested in keeping a Guinea pig outdoors, or even in a garage or basement, you need to ask yourself if you really want a pet at all. Pets are intended to be companions, and companions are intended to keep you company. So why have a pet that doesn't live with you?

Guinea pigs are very susceptible to extremes in temperature, which makes outdoor living hazardous for them. They do not tolerate the heat or exhaust fumes in a garage very well, either. The cold dampness in a basement is likely to make a Guinea pig sick. So it's best to keep your Guinea pig in the house, where you can enjoy him the most.

Adult-supervised care and handling should be the strict rule, but children can learn much about gentleness, compassion, and responsibility when they are involved in caring for the family's pet Guinea pig. Other pets, too, can learn to respect the Guinea pig and his space so they do not harass him. When you give your Guinea pig his own secure place in your home, where he can hear and see people every day, he will grow more and more tame and his personality will blossom.

RESPONSIBLE PET OWNERSHIP

Being a responsible pet owner obviously involves taking proper care of your pet. Are you willing to invest the time to feed, provide fresh water, and perform housekeeping duties for a Guinea pig? Are you willing to spend time every day handling and interacting with your Guinea pig? Proper care also means giving your Guinea pig veterinary attention when necessary. Even though your Guinea pig doesn't cost much to feed and care for, are you prepared for any required veterinary expenses for your furry friend?

Responsible pet ownership also involves being respectful of others. There are many people who are not fond of rodent-type pets. By all means, show off your lovely piggy to friends and guests who are curious, but respect those who are not enamored of Guinea pigs by forgoing an introduction to them.

Finally, before you make a final decision to get any pet, you should check your local ordinances to find out what rules your community has established concerning pet ownership. Some communities do not allow any type of rodent species as pets. When you respect the wishes of others and abide by the law, everyone is happier.

Such respect has made it possible for us to cherish many different types of animal companions. The more people practice responsible pet ownership, the more accepted pet ownership will be, and that creates a win-win situation for both animals and people!

Choosing to adopt a Guinea pig is just the beginning. You'll have many more decisions to make once your piggy friend comes home. Having decided that you are a "Guinea pig person," you can look forward to a life that is much more fun and interesting because you have a piggy in it!

CHAPTER TWO

Guinea Pig History and Breeds

The Guinea pig, with its pearly eyes and crinkled ears, was destined to delight humans from the very beginning. This tailless rodent has more than its cute looks going for it: a lot of personality is packed into its small body. Even so, the Guinea pig's relationship with humans did not start out as that of a pet. Historically, the Guinea pig

This photo from a Peruvian Guinea pig farm shows a variety of Guinea pig breeds.

occupied a position in human culture that was more akin to livestock.

HISTORY

Guinea pigs originated in the Andean region of Peru in South America, where these creatures were domesticated by the Incas about five thousand years ago. Guinea pigs were not valued for their sweet personality and companionship qualities at that time, however. They were considered a source of food, and they were also used in religious and healing ceremonies. The Guinea pig still serves these purposes in some parts of South America.

Spanish explorers arrived in the Andes during the sixteenth century,

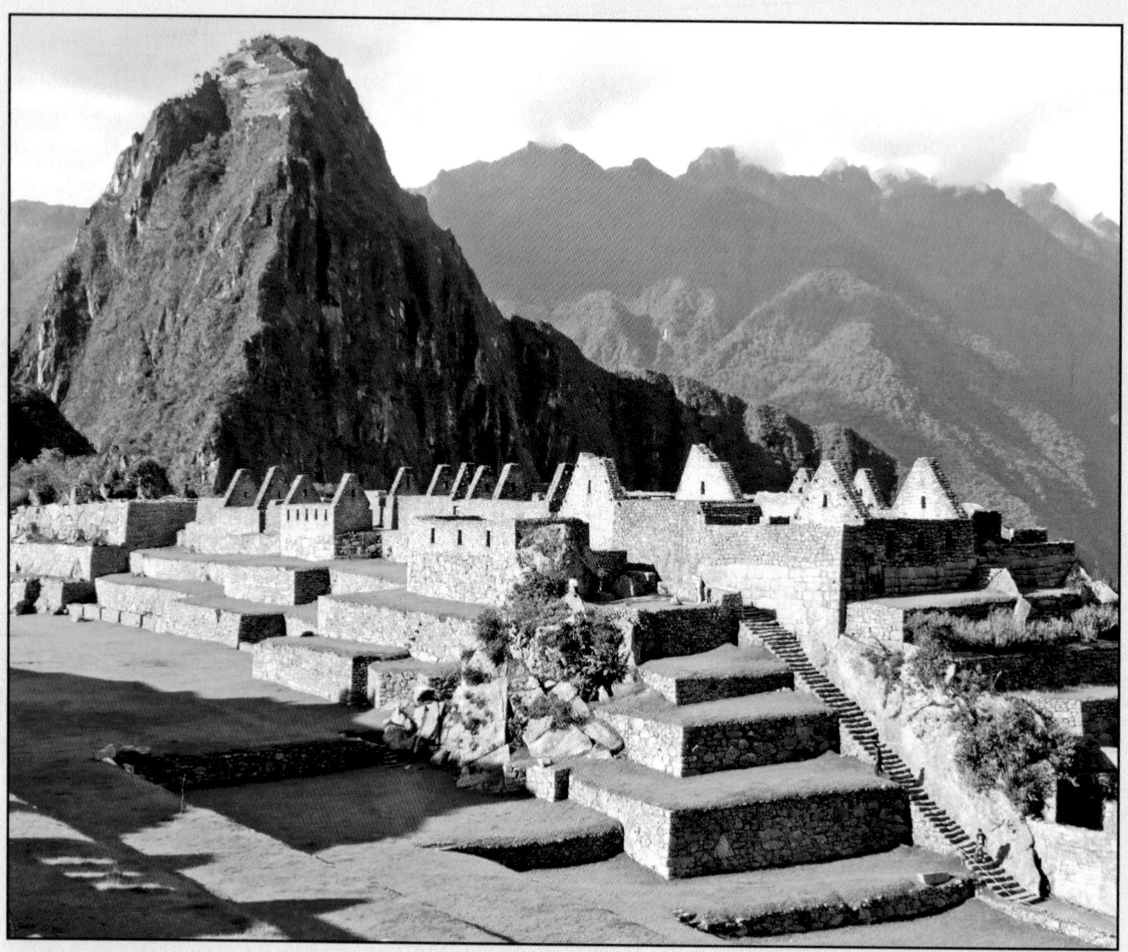

Native Americans living in the mountainous region of South America that today is Peru domesticated Guinea pigs around 5,000 B.C. This photo shows an Incan city, where Guinea pigs would have been raised as food.

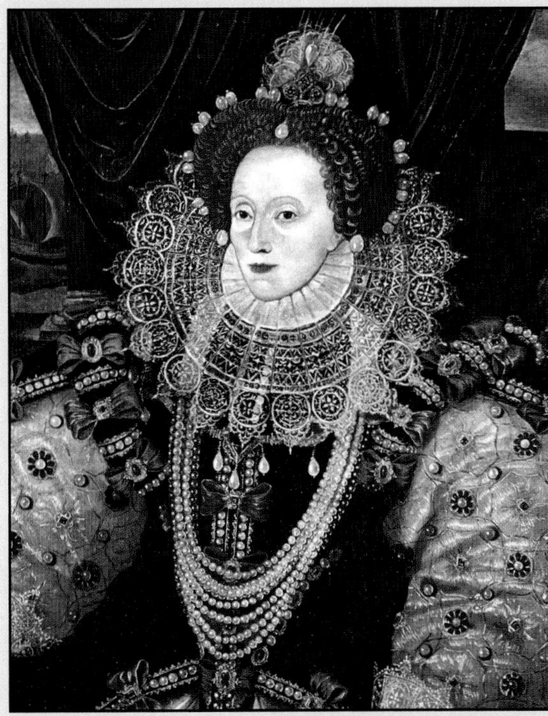

Queen Elizabeth I, who ruled from 1558 to 1603, was a famous guinea pig owner.

and after the Spanish conquest of the Incas in 1532, traders began to bring Guinea pigs back to Europe. These enchanting animals quickly caught on as exotic pets, and it wasn't long before selective breeding began to produce a variety of intriguing characteristics in the species. The charms of this adorable creature were not lost on the nobility of the time. Even Queen Elizabeth I of England is said to have owned one. The imprimatur of royals most certainly boosted the Guinea pig's popularity throughout Europe.

British settlers in the American colonies brought the first Guinea pigs to North America. These pleasingly personable creatures whistled their way into the hearts of Americans and eventually became popular on this side of the Atlantic.

Dog showing was all the rage in both Britain and the United States by the late 1800s, and the showing of cavies (and other small animals) followed suit by the early 1900s. National clubs that governed the showing of small animals went through an evolutionary process, beginning with the National Pet Stock Association in 1920. This organization took charge of shows featuring cavies, rabbits, and hamsters. Eventually, the American Rabbit Breeders Association (ARBA) rose to the task of governing shows for both rabbits and cavies, a job the organization continues to do today.

HAIR VERSUS FUR

Even though the Guinea pig's size and shape have remained relatively unchanged over thousands of years, domestication and selective breeding have produced some dramatic variations in the Guinea pig's coat type and colors. Perhaps because the Guinea pig's natural hair is so coarse, or because the long-haired varieties seem to have such human-like hair, there is an ongoing debate about whether Guinea pigs possess hair or fur.

Scientifically, there is no difference between hair and fur. Both are made of keratin, the same substance in fingernails, feathers, and skin. Even though the hair on different species—or even on different parts of the body of the same species—has different qualities, it is all made of the same stuff. Some hair grows to a certain length, like the hair on your arms, and some hair grows continuously, like the hair on your head.

Different shaft widths give hair different strengths and textures, and it is common to refer to those with thicker shafts as hair, and those with thinner shafts as fur—thus, an elephant has hair while a lion has fur. But there is no real distinction between hair and fur, so you can use whichever term suits you.

There is, however, a widespread misconception that some people who are allergic to animals can tolerate hair better than fur. In fact, allergies are not caused by hair at all, but rather by the dander and other secretions of the animal (including skin oils and saliva) that stick to the hair. Obviously, Guinea pigs do not shed as much hair as dogs do. And cavies are not known for drooling (unless they are sick). These factors may reduce the likelihood of an allergic reaction in some people who are otherwise sensitive to pet dander.

Whether or not a Guinea pig is the ideal pet for a person with allergies really depends on the person's sensitivity. If you suffer from any type of pet allergies, always spend some time with a Guinea pig first, to make sure you can tolerate this

Guinea pigs were first used in biological experiments in the 1600s, but using the term *Guinea pig* to refer to human test subjects did not become common until the first half of the 1900s. Fortunately for the Guinea pig, he has largely been replaced by rats and mice in scientific laboratories! (This photo of scientists injecting a Guinea pig with an experimental vaccine was taken in 1935.)

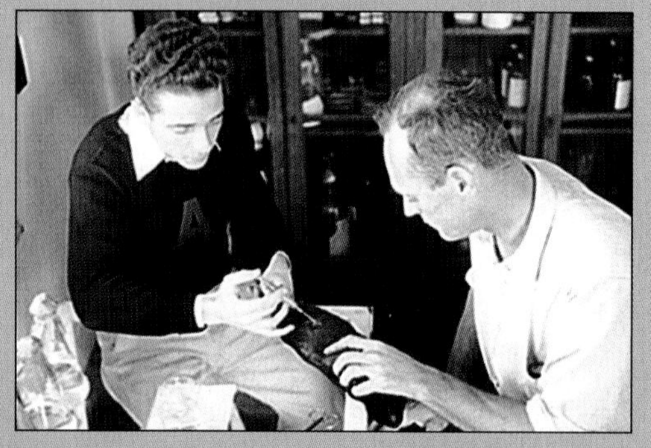

species. When in doubt, it is best not to bring a Guinea pig home.

COLOR CHARACTERISTICS

Guinea pigs come in a rainbow of colors, but these colors are expressed in different ways. Some breeds have a specific color or pattern of colors, while other breeds come in a huge variety of colors. The following terms are used to describe the various color characteristics of Guinea pigs.

AGOUTI: The agouti is a hair color characterized by a darker base coat with guard hairs (longer hairs) that are tipped with a lighter color. This is a hair quality that is also found among wild Guinea pigs. While this gives wild Guinea pigs a camouflaging grayish color (a good defense against predators that have limited color vision), domestic Guinea pigs come in several varieties of agouti. Besides the typical silver, there are golden and dilute agoutis. Dilute agoutis come in several base coat colors (beige, black, chocolate, and lilac) with different combinations of hair tip and eye colors.

This dilute agouti's coat combines beige and dark hairs.

BRINDLE: Brindle is a unique color pattern that combines red and black intermixed hairs. The dominant color may be either red or black, with the alternate color dispersed evenly throughout the coat. This color can appear patchy where the intermingling of colors is not perfectly even, but for show-quality cavies, this is not desirable.

DALMATIAN: The Dalmatian Guinea pig sports a varying pattern of spots over a white body, just like a Dalmatian dog. The spots of this eye-catching coat pattern can be in any recognized Guinea pig color, but the spots must all be the same color.

DUTCH: Dutch Guinea pigs have a marked color pattern, similar to Dutch rabbits. They possess a bright white blaze on the face and a white band around the front half of their bodies. The head and rear half of the body is of the same color, which can be any one of a number of acceptable self, solid, or agouti colors.

HIMALAYAN: The Himalayan's marked pattern consists of dark points on the nose, ears, legs, and feet, which contrast strongly with its white body. Resembling a Himalayan rabbit or a Siamese cat, this breed is exceptionally attractive.

MARKED: The marked pattern refers to those Guinea pigs that display a particular color pattern involving two or more colors. The different-colored patches must be clear-cut and distinct, without any intermingling of different-colored hairs. A broken color Guinea pig refers to any marked Guinea pig that does not conform to a specific patch pattern. Marked Guinea pigs that are subject to specific patch patterns or additional color requirements include the Dutch, Himalayan, Dalmatian, Tortoiseshell, and Tortoiseshell and White.

ROAN: Who says the Guinea pig can share colors only with dogs, cats, and rabbits? Roan, a common color for horses, is also very fashionable for Guinea pigs. This color type consists of white hairs that are interspersed among one or two other colors. Acceptable color companions for the white roan hairs include any of the self, agouti, or solid colors. The "roaning" effect is often heavier behind the shoulders, resulting in a lighter shade on the rear part of the body.

The Dutch Guinea pig has a distinctive white blaze on the face and a white band around the front part of its body.

SELF: A self is a Guinea pig that has a short coat in a solid, uniform color over its entire body. Black and brown (chocolate) are very common self colors. Other self colors include beige, cream, lilac (light gray with a purple cast), red, and white. There is also a self color for show cavies called "red-eyed orange," which describes a cavy with a reddish-orange coat and pink eyes.

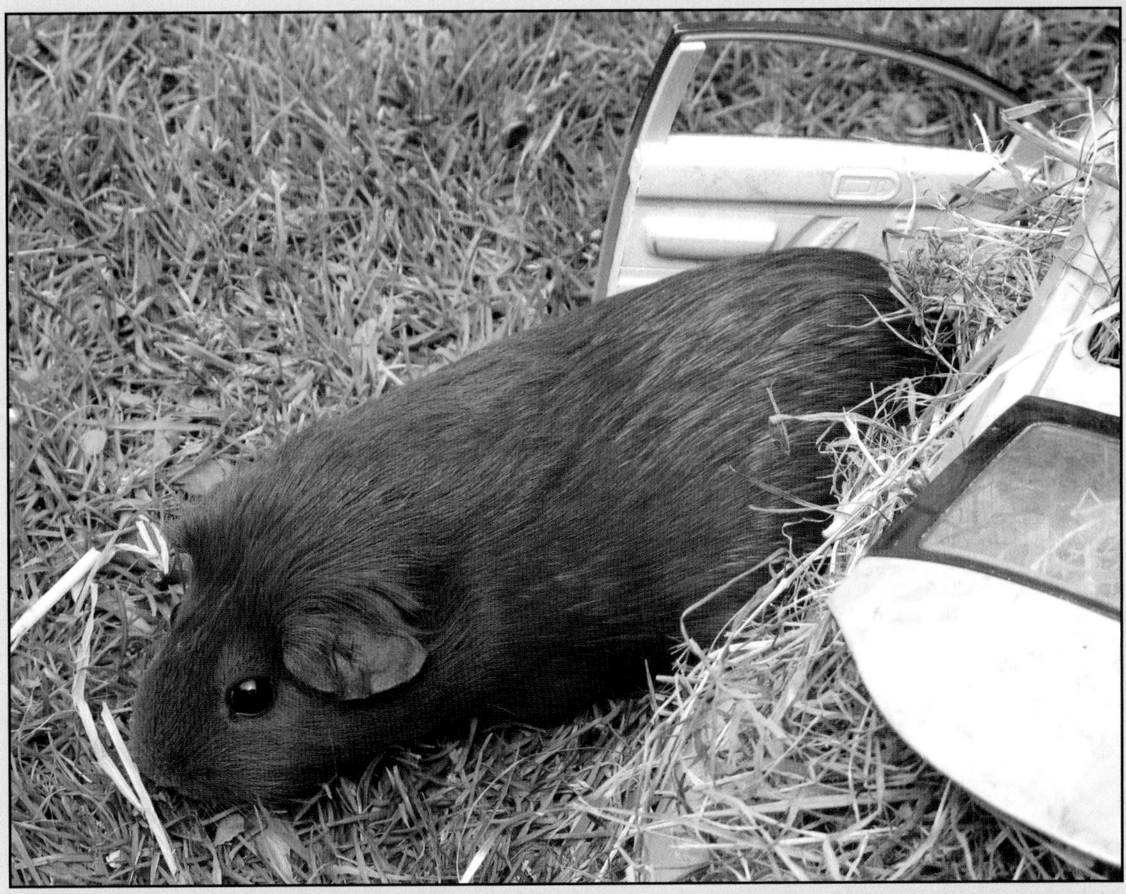

This red self Guinea pig is playing with a toy car.

SOLID: The solid is distinguished from the self by the different-colored hairs intermingled throughout the body. The mixing of hairs this way gives the impression of a solid color, even thought the hairs are of different colors. (The brindle, which possesses black and red hairs, is considered a solid, even though its coat may sometimes appear to have black or red patchy areas.) These patches, upon closer examination, are not pure black or red, as there is some intermixing of the complementary color in them.

TORTOISESHELL: Just like a tortoiseshell cat, the tortoiseshell Guinea pig is dressed in patches of red and black. For show purposes, these patches should be in a checkerboard pattern and distributed equally on the body. This coordinated and balanced color pattern is definitely

FAST FACT

The dark markings on the Himalayan Guinea pig's nose, ears, and feet are heat sensitive. They can appear lighter in warm weather and darker in cold weather.

appealing, but the tortoiseshell and white takes the prize for flashiness.

Tortoiseshell and White: If you really want attention, add some chrome. When you put a few patches of white on a tortoiseshell Guinea pig, the added sparkle is undeniable. Similar to the color of a calico cat, the tortoiseshell and white Guinea pig comes in a truly attractive package. For a show-quality cavy, the patches of color must be clearly defined and in a checkerboard pattern. A dividing line runs down the middle of the back and another line goes around the middle of the body, separating the body into boldly colored quarters.

Satin: Satin isn't really a color, but it is a coat quality that deserves special mention. Satin Guinea pigs possess a distinctive sheen to their coats, thanks to the hollow, translucent quality of their hair shafts. This trait has been bred into the majority of cavy breeds recognized by the ARBA. Because it is a different coat type, like long hair or short hair, satins are classified as separate breeds. For example, there are American Satins, Abyssinian Satins, and Peruvian Satins. There are satin types of other breeds as well.

BREEDS

There are thirteen breeds of cavy currently recognized by the ARBA. All these breeds have distinctive and delightful characteristics. Due to their different physical features, they do have different care requirements, especially when it comes to the maintenance of their coats. This is something to keep in mind when deciding which breed will fit your lifestyle best.

Abyssinian: The Abyssinian, one of the oldest Guinea pig breeds, is easy to recognize by the rosettes that cover his entire body. Each rosette has a center point from which the hair grows outward, like a starburst. These rosettes must form a certain pattern on purebred cavies, and there must be at least eight of them (ten is preferred) to be shown. There is a rosette on each shoulder, four around the barrel of the body, one on each hip, and two on the rear. A distinctive ridge pattern forms where these rosettes butt up against each other. In order to maintain their rosette shapes, the Abyssinian's hair is necessarily coarse. He comes in a variety of colors and makes quite a conversation piece with his unusual hairstyle.

ABYSSINIAN SATIN: The Abyssinian Satin has the same physical characteristics as the Abyssinian, except that it has the signature shiny coat of a Satin.

AMERICAN: The most common domestic Guinea pig is the American (called the "English" in England). His short, dense coat comes in a great variety of solid or mixed colors. This type of coat is straight and sleek, giving the appearance of always being perfectly groomed. With a coat that is the easiest to maintain by far, the American is understandably one of the most popular pet breeds.

AMERICAN SATIN: The American Satin has the same physical characteristics as the American, except for the coat texture. In contrast to the American's coarse fur, the Satin's coat is finer, shinier, and softer, and feels as smooth as satin.

CORONET: The Coronet is the newest long-haired breed. It has the added feature of a rosette on its forehead. This rosette elongates with age so that

The multidirectional hair growth of the Abyssinian (shown here) and Abyssinian Satin breeds results in a facial feature called a "mustache." This feature must be well developed in a show cavy.

it droops over the eyes and extends to the mane just above the ears—thus the name Coronet (crown). The rest of its long hair grows back toward the rear without a part, which exposes its adorably cute face.

Peruvian: If you love long tresses, a Peruvian has lots of luscious locks. The first long-haired breed, the Peruvian does require more coat maintenance than a short-haired Guinea pig. The hair grows forward over the Guinea pig's face and fans out around the rest of his body, giving him the appearance of a wig with legs. The hair is parted down the middle of the back and can grow to over a foot (30.5 cm) in length. Show cavies usually have their hair divided into sections and wrapped in small pieces of cloth or paper towels to protect it from dirt and breakage. Members of this breed are not considered practical pets for most people, but their hair can be trimmed for easier upkeep.

Peruvian Satin: The Peruvian Satin sports the same luxuriously long coat as the Peruvian, but it has the highly coveted satiny sheen and silky texture characteristic of the other Satin breeds.

Silkie: The Silkie, called the "Sheltie" in England, is another long-haired breed that is distinguished from the Peruvian by hair that grows back and away from the face. The

The Silkie Guinea pig has a distinctive long coat of hair.

hair is not parted down the back. Instead, it forms a mane around the head and gives the Guinea pig a teardrop appearance from above. The Silkie acquired its name by virtue of the soft, silky feel of its coat.

Silkie Satin: The Silkie Satin looks the same as the Silkie, with the added gloss of its Satin hair.

Teddy: The Teddy, called the "Rex" in England, is "fuzzy looking" (like a teddy bear), just as its name implies. Its short, plush coat is frizzy but not curly. The hair texture is coarse and resilient. If pressed down, it will rise back up to its erect position. The Teddy comes in any of the accepted Guinea pig colors and patterns, and can become quite a conversation piece pet.

Physical Feature Glossary

back ridge: the ridge of hair formed down the middle of the back on Abyssinian breeds.

banded: when a single color completely encircles the body.

blaze: a broad white stripe down the front of the face.

cheek sweeps: the hair that grows from the side of the face on longhaired cavies.

collar: also called a "ruff," this term refers to the ridge of hair across the shoulders of the Abyssinian breeds.

coronet: the elongated crest on the forehead of the Coronet breed.

crest: the rosette on the head of the White Crested breed.

frontal: hair that falls forward over the face of the Peruvian breeds.

rear sweep: hair that falls over the hindquarters of a longhaired cavy.

resiliency: a hair quality that causes the hair to return to an erect position, such as that found in the Teddy breeds.

rosette: hair that radiates outward from a center point.

rump ridge: also called a "rear ruff," this refers to the ridge of hair that runs across the rear area of the Abyssinian breeds.

side sweeps: the hair that extends out from the sides of longhaired cavies.

smut: also called a "smudge," this term refers to the sooty appearance of a color marking.

ticking: when the guard hair color matches the undercoat color.

tipping: refers to the color of the hair tips, when that color is different from the color on the rest of the hair shaft.

FAST FACT

Due to recessive genes, Roan and Dalmatian Guinea pigs should always be bred to self-colored Guinea pigs rather than their own kind, because there is a risk of producing white offspring that are lethally deformed.

TEDDY SATIN: The Teddy Satin looks identical to the Teddy, but its coat has the glow of a Satin breed.

TEXEL: The Texel is a very distinctive-looking Guinea pig, and some people might wonder what planet it came from. Its long, thick hair cascades in beautiful, tiny curls. The Texel can have hair that falls in either ringlet-type curls or corkscrews. Both are equally desirable. Unlike the Teddy, the Texel's coat is not kinky or coarse, but rather, soft and silky. But be forewarned that such beauty has a price. This is probably the highest-maintenance hairdo in Guinea pigdom!

WHITE CRESTED: Like the Coronet, the White Crested has a hair variation on its face. A single white rosette (crest) appears on its forehead. This is the only white spot on its entire body. Its body coat is short and smooth, and can be any color or combination of colors that does not include white.

OTHER VARIETIES OF GUINEA PIGS

Breeders seem to be on a never-ending journey to create new and interesting varieties of Guinea pigs. There are many Guinea pig types that are not yet accepted as breeds by the ARBA or the British Cavy Council (BCC), but they are still gaining a lot of attention nonetheless.

In America, hairless Guinea pigs have developed into a noticeable population. The Baldwin Guinea pig is completely hairless as an adult. The Skinny Pig, by contrast, often has some hair on the face and feet that make its body seem "skinny." While they are not the most cuddly or attractive pigs, they definitely fulfill a fetish for something bizarre or different!

The Merino, which has the long hair and crest of a Coronet, is distinguished by its wavy hair. The Alpaca, which resembles a curly-haired Peruvian, is also gaining popularity.

In the United Kingdom, the Rare Varieties Cavy Club promotes a number of new colors and coat types for Guinea pigs. The Ridgeback is a shorthaired cavy with a well-defined ridge of hair that runs the length of its back. The Magpie has a half-white and half-black face, with balanced patches of white, black, and a white/black mix over the body. The Belted has an unusual color pattern that includes a white belt around the entire body behind the shoulder.

GUINEA PIG ORGANIZATIONS

In order for a new variety of Guinea pig to be accepted as a breed, the genetic traits of the Guinea pig must be able to breed true in every generation. If some of the offspring of two curly-haired Guinea pigs turn out to have short, straight hair, they are not breeding true for the curly-haired characteristic. It can take many, many generations to produce a genetically predictable strain. Predictability in appearance is what gives a breed its identity and distinguishes it from other breeds.

National organizations are responsible for registering purebred Guinea pigs and making decisions about accepting new breeds. In the United States, Canada, and Mexico, the American Rabbit Breeders Association performs these functions. In the United Kingdom, the British Cavy Council has assumed these responsibilities.

American Rabbit Breeders Association (ARBA): Earlier in its history, the ARBA was known as the American Rabbit and Cavy Breeders Association, but cavy breeders elected to separate into their own organization in 1952. The American Cavy Breeders Association (ACBA) and the ARBA have since reunited. Rather than combining their names, each remains a separate entity, with the ACBA functioning as a division of the ARBA.

The ARBA remains the leading authority on rabbits and cavies in America. The association publishes an in-depth guide, titled *The Standard of Perfection*, which includes conformation standards for all official rabbit and cavy breeds. This guide, which should be in every serious cavy fancier's library, is updated every five years to include information on newly accepted breeds.

The ARBA is also responsible for sanctioning rabbit and cavy shows and holds a national convention and show

once a year. This organization provides support for all types of rabbit and cavy owners, including pet owners, fanciers, and commercial breeders. The association's Web site, www.arba.net, can provide more information on ARBA's services.

British Cavy Council (BCC): The BCC is the leading authority on cavies in the UK. It is responsible for the registration of purebred cavies, establishing standards for the judging of cavies at shows, and approving any new breeds of cavies. Unlike the ARBA, however, the BCC is not involved in sanctioning shows. Shows are generally governed by regional cavy clubs throughout the UK.

The purpose of the BCC is strictly to provide consistent standards and a central registration source for cavy clubs. Any matter that affects the general interests of cavy owners is also brought to the council's attention. Because the functions of the BCC are limited and it does not maintain a membership per se (it consists only of a board of directors), cavy fanciers in the UK who are interested in showing their cavies must join a local or regional breed club.

The National Cavy Club (NCC) maintains a Web site at www.nationalcavyclub.co.uk with a directory of club links. This is the best place to start when you're looking for a Guinea pig club in the United Kingdom.

The marvelously diverse physical characteristics of the Guinea pig have fascinated fanciers for hundreds of years. Regardless of how he looks on the outside, however, it's the inside that holds the greatest treasure. With such a wonderful personality, it's no wonder the Guinea pig evolved from a domesticated food source to a cherished pet!

CHAPTER THREE

Finding the Right Guinea Pig

If you had any preconceived ideas about what a Guinea pig should look like, you may be both overwhelmed and excited to discover the great variety of features that characterize this species. Besides the very different physical features of purebred cavies, there is even more diversification among mixed breeds. Let this fact remind you that each Guinea pig is as much an individual on the inside as it is on the outside.

Choosing a Guinea pig involves much more than deciding which physical features are attractive to you. You need to choose a Guinea pig that is in good health, has a personality you will enjoy, and will fit

Although some types of Guinea pigs may look alike, they can have very different personalities and temperaments.

into your life as either a pet or a show animal. Obtaining your Guinea pig from a quality source is the first step.

WHERE TO FIND A GUINEA PIG

A Guinea pig will inherit characteristics from its parents, but it will also be a product of its environment. When both the nature and nurture of a Guinea pig's upbringing are of good quality, the Guinea pig itself will also be of good quality.

Shelters or Rescues: If you are simply looking for a good pet, there are many adorable Guinea pigs available for adoption through animal shelters and cavy rescues. You might find some purebreds here, but for the most part adoptable Guinea pigs are custom-designed mixed breeds. The assortment of colors and personalities offers much to choose from, and best of all, the adoption fees are usually very affordable.

The only disadvantage of getting a pet from a source like this is that it is difficult to determine the Guinea pig's history. It can be hard to tell exactly how old an adult pig is, and there is no way to know how the animal was treated or handled before it became homeless. Fortunately, most shelters and rescues are very diligent about evaluating their adoptable animals and can give you some insights into each animal's habits and behaviors.

If a local animal shelter does not have any Guinea pigs available for adoption, check the petfinder.com Web site for adoptable cavies

It's OK to be choosy—make sure that you pick the Guinea pig that is right for you!

in your area. This Web site maintains a database of adoptable animals all across the country.

FAST FACT

Some Guinea pigs do not have much affinity for humans, which means they don't particularly enjoy being touched or handled. This may be due to a lack of socialization when the pig was young, or there could be a genetic component that makes some pigs naturally wilder than others. When given the choice, always select personality over looks.

Breeders: If you are interested in showing and breeding your Guinea pig, or you have your heart set on a specific breed of Guinea pig, you should obtain your stock from a reputable breeder. Local and national cavy clubs can provide information on member breeders. You can also find breeders by attending local cavy shows.

Keep in mind that membership in a club does not automatically guarantee that someone is a reputable breeder. You need to physically inspect the breeding operation. Some of the things to look for include cleanliness, condition of the breeder's stock, and the temperament of the animals. If the housing area for the Guinea pigs has a strong ammonia odor or the pens are noticeably filthy, you can assume the breeder does not devote enough time to the proper care of her animals or their facilities.

The Guinea pigs should appear clean, robust, and active. If any one of the Guinea pigs in a litter shows signs of illness, all of the breeder's stock may be infected with an illness or parasite. Keep in mind that Guinea pigs that seem excessively wild or fearful may not have received much handling. Handling young Guinea pigs is crucial to socializing them to humans.

A reputable breeder should be able to provide records of her animals' lineage and health. If the Guinea pigs are registered as purebreds, registrations papers should also be available. Baby Guinea pigs should not leave their mothers until they are at least four weeks old.

A good breeder is not only a source of quality Guinea pigs; she can also be a good source of information if you should run into problems or have questions about your pet. She might even become a mentor or a valuable ally if you decide to show your Guinea pig. So choose your breeder wisely and have the courage to walk away if a breeder does not appear to meet your standards or expectations.

Pet Shops: Many pet stores offer Guinea pigs for sale, just as they do hamsters, mice, and other rodent pets. Sometimes this source can be the best bet for a newcomer to Guinea pig keeping, because the shop staff can set you up with all the supplies you need to get started, preferably in a package deal.

Although it's nice to get a good deal on cages, bedding, food, and other supplies, don't skimp on the quality of your Guinea pig. The same criterion that applies to choosing a good breeder also applies to choosing a good pet shop. The animals should be kept in clean conditions, they should appear to be in good health, and records should be available to determine the animal's age and health status.

Pet shops often obtain their animals from commercial breeders or pet owners who allowed their pets to breed, so don't expect to find show-quality cavies here. Still, they can be just as lovable as any other pet piggy. Just be sure to ask for a health guarantee!

Regardless of where you obtain your Guinea pig, always ask about health guarantees—and get them in writing!

Internet: The Internet is a great tool for locating adoptable Guinea pigs or Guinea pigs for sale. You can easily check the Web sites of local shelters to see if they have any Guinea pigs available. Breeders will often announce the arrival of new litters via their Web sites.

Searching for your Guinea pig online can save you plenty of time and travel expense. However, you should never purchase a Guinea pig without inspecting the animal and its environment. Although there are some breeders who are willing to ship their animals long distances, traveling is stressful for Guinea pigs and can result in illness or death. When health problems are discovered, it can also be difficult to obtain a remedy from a breeder who is located in another state. So limit your search to a reasonable distance from your home and never purchase a Guinea pig sight unseen.

CHOOSING A GUINEA PIG

Now that you know where to go hunting for your special piggy friend, how do you know which Guinea pig is the right one? If cuteness were the deciding factor, you'd have to take them all home! Even if you've already decided on the type and color of Guinea pig you like the best, which sex should you choose? Should you adopt more than one? Does individual temperament matter? Considering each of these factors can help you choose the perfect Guinea pig companion.

Temperament: Each Guinea pig is an individual, and getting to know your Guinea pig's personality is part of the fun of cavy ownership. Your Guinea pig might prefer carrots over celery. He might like to be scratched behind the ears. He might like to run in wild circles in his cage once a day for exercise. You can find out what makes your particular Guinea pig "tick" simply by observing him, petting different parts of his body, or offering him different kinds of fresh greens or vegetables to eat.

There really aren't any "bad" personality traits in the Guinea pig world, just as there is not a Guinea pig on earth that has a mean bone in

You may be able to find a pet Guinea pig on the Internet, if there is no breeder near your home. Rescue organizations often list available Guinea pigs on their Web sites.

Watching to see how young Guinea pigs interact with each other at the breeder's farm or in a pet shop can help you pick the piggy with the right temperament for you and your family.

its body. This species is genetically programmed to be gentle and skittish. But it's the "skittish" part that can cause problems in their interactions with humans. Almost all Guinea pigs will naturally try to escape when you attempt to pick them up, but those that have become accustomed to handling will settle immediately in their owner's arms.

If you want a tame animal that you can hold, carry, pet, and play with, it is imperative that you spend time handling your Guinea pig frequently. Like many other domesticated animals, Guinea pigs can become almost feral from a lack of human contact. Ideally, you should choose a Guinea pig that is already comfortable with human handling. It is very difficult to tend to a Guinea pig's needs—like trimming its nails, grooming, or administering medications—if it won't tolerate handling.

PHYSICAL CHARACTERISTICS: Whether you want a pet or a show prospect, you need to choose a healthy Guinea pig. In addition to checking the eyes, nose, and skin for signs of illness or parasites, you must also check the Guinea pig's feet for

While inspecting a Guinea pig, if you notice that the animal is shedding some hair, don't be alarmed. Guinea pigs go through shedding cycles, just like cats and dogs. Hair loss is only a concern if it is accompanied by bare spots, skin lesions, or external parasites like fleas or lice.

injuries. Comb through the animal's fur with your fingers to feel for any lumps that might be abscesses, scabs, or scars. Check the Guinea pig's mouth for sores that may indicate overgrown or misaligned teeth.

Show prospects require even more rigorous scrutiny. You should become thoroughly familiar with the conformation standards of the breed that has caught your fancy. Guinea pigs may all appear basically the same, but there are some minor differences in size, shape of the nose, and other physical characteristics that apply to each of the breeds. Be sure to obtain expert advice in choosing a show pig.

MALE OR FEMALE?: Like other animals that live in social groups, Guinea pigs are happiest when they live in the

GUINEA PIG COMMUNICATION

Verbal

purring: very similar to a cat's purr, it is a sign of contentment and relaxation.

rumbling: a deep purr used in the seduction of a mate, or to warn rivals of impending aggression.

squeal: a warning or an indication of fear or pain. Guinea pigs sometimes squeal quite loudly when they beg for food—they won't let you forget about feeding time!

teeth chattering: this is a warning to other Guinea pigs of impending aggression.

whistle: not quite as loud as a squeal, a whistle indicates that a Guinea pig wants attention. Sometimes Guinea pigs whistle a haphazard melody with high/low and loud/soft whistles as if they were talking to themselves.

Body Language

direct stare: a sign of dominance aggression, often accompanied by raised hackles and a verbal warning.

jumping: a sign of excitement and happiness.

nose nuzzle: a friendly greeting to another Guinea pig.

stiff front legs: a sign of dominance aggression, often accompanied by a verbal warning.

Some Guinea pigs are able to get along well with other piggies. However, a few won't be as willing to share their food or living space.

company of their own kind. However, boars (males) tend to tolerate solitary life better than sows (females). If you are going to own a single Guinea pig, a boar is recommended.

If you plan to double your fun with two Guinea pigs, sows are known to have fewer squabbles between them. Two boars can become quite bonded to each other, too, if they are raised with each other and there are no sows around to fuel the fires of sexual competition. In the interest of avoiding a pet overpopulation problem in your own home, it is not a good idea to house a boar and sow together unless one or both of them is surgically neutered (see Neutering and Spaying in chapter 6). Even serious breeders keep the sexes separated to limit reproduction.

Adhering to these guidelines does not always guarantee harmonious relationships between Guinea pigs, as the success of any relationship depends on the personalities involved. A human can't expect to get along with every single person on earth, and you can't expect your Guinea pig to get along with all other Guinea pigs, either. Personality conflicts are just as common in the Guinea pig world. When conflicts are too frequent or serious, you may have to separate the combatants.

Guinea pigs of either sex that are raised together can become quite bonded to each other, but if you are introducing two strange adult Guinea pigs to each other, you need to do it gradually. Keep them in two separate cages next to each other so they will have a chance to get used to each other's scent and presence. You can also put them in the same cage with a divider to separate them. When they seem to be tolerating each other quite well, you can place them together in neutral territory—someplace unfamiliar to both of them. A large cardboard box works very well for this.

Some squabbles among Guinea pigs are normal—that's part of how they communicate with each other and establish a natural "pecking order." Guinea pigs can make some pretty horrendous noises when they are irritated, but their bark is usually bigger than their bite. If the disagreements between your Guinea pigs do not dissipate quickly, or if they result in nasty bites and injuries, it is best to assume the relationship was not meant to be.

FAST FACT

When they are excited, Guinea pigs will sometimes pop straight into the air into a flip that lands them on their feet. This amusing bit of athletics is called popcorning.

Searching for the right Guinea pig can be a fun adventure, but it can also be disappointing and frustrating when the "right" Guinea pig doesn't materialize as soon as your search begins. Be patient! There is a Guinea pig out there for you, and you will never regret holding out for just the right one.

CHAPTER FOUR

The Best Possible Beginning

Guinea pigs have entertained generations of humans with their winning antics. They have endeared themselves to us with their adorably cute countenance. And they have bonded with us in unique ways. No doubt you are looking forward to enjoying Guinea pig ownership for these same reasons.

All these benefits can only come from a happy, healthy Guinea pig—one that has been raised and cared for properly. Being prepared to provide your new pet with the necessary

Before you bring a Guinea pig home, make sure that the entire family knows the rules with regard to proper handling and care.

care and handling from the very beginning will ensure that you and your new friend will develop a wonderful long-term relationship.

THE CAGE

Your Guinea pig will require a home of his own, where he can feel safe and secure. There are many different types of small animal cages on the market, but they are not all appropriate for Guinea pigs. Look for a cage with a solid bottom rather than a wire-mesh bottom. A wire-mesh floor may make it easier to clean your pet's cage, but it can also be injurious to your Guinea pig's soft, padded feet.

The bars or wire mesh of the cage should be close enough together to keep your Guinea pig from squeezing through, and the entry door should be secure enough to keep your Guinea pig in and other pets out. The mesh needs to be constructed of 16- or 18-gauge wire. This means that chicken wire, nylon netting, or insect screening are out, as they can be gnawed by the Guinea pig or cause safety hazards.

A large glass aquarium can make a good cage, provided there is sufficient air circulation. Avoid aquariums that are too deep, and be careful where the aquarium is placed. Any direct sunlight can turn an aquarium into a stifling hot greenhouse that can kill your Guinea pig. A Guinea pig is not likely to escape

A large fish tank like this can provide a nice home for your Guinea pig.

from an open-top aquarium, but the aquarium will still need to be fitted with a wire-mesh cover that snaps or locks in place to protect your Guinea pig from any other household pets.

If you prefer to give your Guinea pig a luxury suite with a loft, there are plenty of pet cages on the market that feature multiple levels. Guinea pigs are not athletic climbers, so ramps should not be too steep. Removable ramps and lofts are ideal because they can be taken down to give your pet more room if he shows no interest in using an upper level.

One of the most important considerations when choosing a Guinea pig cage is size. In most cases, bigger is better; more room gives your Guinea a chance for more exercise. If you plan to litter box train your piggy, you'll need enough room in the cage for a small litter box, while still leaving room for your pet to move about. But you do need to be practical—remember, you have to clean it! At a minimum, a cage for a single Guinea pig should be at least eighteen by thirty inches (46 x 76 cm). Cages can be quite expensive, so if you'd like to give your pet room to roam, consider constructing your own Guinea pig pen.

The best place for your pet's cage is on a table that puts the cage at waist height. This makes it much easier to care for your Guinea pig. A microwave cart or a small TV stand are ideal, as you can store your pet's food and supplies in the cabinet underneath.

It is important to keep your Guinea pig's cage away from doors and windows, where drafts can make your pet sick. Guinea pigs enjoy the activity, attention, and interaction they get when their cage is located in a main living area, but they do not appreciate an excessive amount of traffic or noise, which can be stressful for them.

A tublike cage that has solid sides four to five inches (10–13 cm) high will help keep food and bedding inside the cage. Guinea pigs are known to get into playful "scurrying" fits that can send the cage contents flying all over the room!

OUTDOOR HUTCH

As stated earlier, the best environment for a Guinea pig is one where the Guinea pig is kept as a household pet. Guinea pigs do not make good outdoor pets. Because of their sensitivity to extremes in temperature, they can become overheated

Guinea pigs can be kept in an outdoor hutch like this one. However, in hot weather you'll have to make sure that your piggy gets plenty of cool water, so he does not suffer from dehydration or heat prostration.

quickly. This species evolved in a temperate climate, and its wild cousins enjoy relatively stable temperatures by living in underground dens. In addition to weather concerns, the outdoor Guinea pig is more susceptible to predators, parasites, and illness.

If you happen to live in a warmer climate and insist on keeping your pet outdoors, a weather-resistant, rabbit-type hutch will be sufficient. You will need to make one modification, however, to prevent injury to your pet's feet. A Guinea pig does not have thick hair on the bottom of its feet, as a rabbit does, to protect its feet from the abrasive wire bottom of a rabbit hutch. So you will have to provide solid flooring throughout much of the hutch to keep your pet comfortable.

The hutch should be located out of direct sunlight and preferably placed near a windbreak, such as a building. Provide as much protection for your outdoor Guinea pig as possible. Even with good care, you can expect an outdoor Guinea pig to have a slightly shorter life span than an indoor pet.

NEST BOX

A home is not very comfortable without furniture, but your Guinea pig has very modest decorating tastes. There is only one amenity he needs to be happy, and that is a nest box. Consider it your Guinea pig's bedroom. He needs someplace to sleep or rest, to retreat from noisy or overstimulating surroundings, and to feel safe when he gets scared.

A good nest box has to be large enough for your Guinea pig to turn around inside comfortably, but it shouldn't be so large that your Guinea pig has to retreat to a corner of it to feel safe. If you want the nest box to last, it should be constructed of wood, as Guinea pigs can be indiscriminately destructive of their own property. If you have an endless supply of shoe boxes, however, you can keep replacing his bedroom as needed.

The nest box should have at least one three-by-three-inch (8 by 8 cm) doorway cut into it. And be sure to provide a separate nest box for each Guinea pig if you own more than one. Your pets shouldn't have to fight for a safe place to retreat!

BEDDING

Bedding is a personal decision. You might want to try out different products to see which one you like the best. Wood shavings, ground corncobs and shredded paper are all acceptable; but do not use cedar shavings, as they are toxic to Guinea pigs. (Commercially packaged bedding that is safe for Guinea pigs is often labeled as such.) Straw and hay are not the best choices, either, as

A wooden nest box provides a sturdy hiding place for your Guinea pig.

Wood chips make good bedding and floor material for your Guinea pig.

your Guinea pig might gnaw on the straw after it has been contaminated with his waste.

To make cage cleanup easier, you can line the bottom of the cage with newspaper. Then, when it's time to change the bedding, you can roll the old bedding up neatly and dispose of it.

FEEDING SUPPLIES

Although a nest box is the only furniture your Guinea pig demands, this does not mean the rest of his living quarters are barren. There are a number of other supplies you will need to stock in order to care for your Guinea pig properly. Food and water are at the top of the list.

FAST FACT

You can help your Guinea pig settle down and adjust to his new home by draping a towel or blanket over a portion of his cage to give him a little more privacy and security for the first week.

Since Guinea pigs have horribly destructive teeth, a metal or crock-style (extra-thick plastic) food dish is recommended. A good size would be three inches (8 cm) in diameter. Any larger, and your Guinea pig might make it a plaything and kick his food all over the cage! Any smaller, and you might have to fill it too frequently. Some Guinea pigs think it is fun to tip their food dishes over and spread food pellets all over their homes (the Guinea pig version of a food fight). In this case, a food dish that attaches to the side of the cage is a good investment.

Guinea pigs can make a real mess of a water dish, too, so you are best off getting a water bottle with a steel ball valve at the end of it. The bottle can be hung upside down on the outside of the cage, which makes changing the water very easy. Again, get a water bottle that is large enough so you don't have to worry about your pet running out of water, and so that you won't have to fill it more than once a day—a twelve-to-sixteen-ounce (350 to 475 ml) capacity is ideal.

A hay rack is optional. This attaches to the side of the cage and keeps your Guinea pig's hay supply clean for consumption. If you don't supply more hay than your Guinea pig will eat at one time, a hay rack really isn't necessary.

SUPPLY CHECKLIST

- Cage or hutch
- Bedding
- Nest box
- Chew blocks
- Food bowl
- Water bottle
- Commercial feed
- Hay
- Fresh greens or vegetables
- Toenail clipper
- Brush or comb
- Pet carrier

OTHER SUPPLIES

It can be quite boring to be confined to a cage for a good portion of every day, so be sure to throw in some toys for your Guinea pig. Chewing items are especially relished by your little friend. Wood chew blocks, cardboard toilet paper rolls, and other safe Guinea pig toys can help banish the boredom and provide good exercise.

You'll also need some items to help you care for your Guinea pig's hygiene. A brush or comb will keep his hair healthy and tangle-free, and a nail clipper will keep his nails from growing too long. If you have a long-haired Guinea pig, a slicker brush (a flat-headed brush with short, thin wire tines) or a pin brush (an oval-headed brush with longer, thicker, flexible tines) are must-haves. Brushing is not so critical for a short-haired Guinea pig, but you can still enjoy bonding with your pet by grooming him. A cat or dog flea comb (a comb with tines that are very close together) will neaten the fine coat of your short-haired piggy.

A human toenail clipper is usually sufficient for clipping Guinea pig nails. If your Guinea pig's nails are too large for a toenail clipper, a small cat or dog nail clipper should do the job.

If you plan to litter box train your Guinea pig, you'll also need a small litter box. This store-bought or homemade box should have a cut-out doorway, as Guinea pigs are not climbers and they need an easy way to access the box. You will only be able to keep this in your Guinea pig's cage if the cage is large enough to accommodate it. Your Guinea pig still has to have some room to play!

Finally, a pet carrier is an absolute must. A small pet carrier comes in handy when you need a safe place to put your Guinea pig while you are cleaning his cage. It is absolutely necessary if you are going to transport your Guinea pig for any reason—to the vet's office, to the pet sitter's, to shows, or when moving.

BRINGING YOUR GUINEA PIG HOME

When the thrilling day has arrived and you are prepared to bring your Guinea pig home, you'll probably be jittery with excitement. Your Guinea pig, however, will probably be jittery with stress. Being placed in a completely new environment will be scary and overwhelming for him. The best thing you can do to help your Guinea pig adjust to his new home is to leave him alone for several days before handling him.

To keep your Guinea pig looking his best, you'll need a small pet brush and clippers to trim his nails.

This is perhaps the hardest part of Guinea pig ownership—to control your excitement over your new pet and to keep things quiet for the first few days. But this is absolutely necessary if you want to prevent your Guinea pig from becoming overly stressed, which can lead to illness and injuries. Leaving him alone will allow your Guinea pig to become accustomed to his new surroundings. In the long run, it will enable your Guinea pig to settle down into his new life much more quickly.

Plenty of chew toys can help provide diversions and stress relief. If you offer a treat of fresh greens or fruit on a regular daily schedule, your Guinea pig will learn very quickly what a wonderful human you are! He'll begin to feel more comfortable with you and will look forward to seeing you at the same time each day. His personality, too, will begin to shine through as he begins to whistle and chatter to you.

HANDLING YOUR GUINEA PIG

When you're ready to begin handling your Guinea pig, you need to know how to pick up, hold, and handle your pet. Too many Guinea pigs are injured or killed due to improper handling. It can be difficult to get hold of your Guinea pig when he is darting about his cage, and when you do finally catch him, it is equally hard to keep your grip on him if he struggles to escape. Here are some techniques that can help you keep control of a skittish new Guinea pig.

With practice, you'll gain confidence in Guinea pig handling. Your Guinea pig, too, will settle down, gain confidence, and become much easier to handle.

Picking up Your Piggy: When attempting to catch your Guinea pig, it is best to do it as quickly as possible to minimize stress to the animal. Relentlessly chasing your Guinea pig about his pen will just escalate his panic. Quickly and firmly reach in and grasp him by the shoulders. If you try to pick him up from underneath, he will use his legs to launch himself off your hand.

Pick your Guinea pig up by the shoulders and immediately support his

FAST FACT

If you choose to keep two or more Guinea pigs, it's not unusual for them to show preference for the company of other Guinea pigs rather than humans. Frequent handling will be required to keep their connection to humans intact.

Handle a Guinea pig gently but firmly, using one hand to support his body and the other to prevent him from jumping or wriggling out of your hand.

backside with your other hand while removing him from his pen—this will give him a sense of security so he won't struggle. You can then bring him close to your body to hold him in your arms. Always keep one hand around your Guinea pig's body while holding him, to prevent him from jumping out of your grasp and falling.

Holding Your Guinea Pig: A hold that is particularly useful to prevent the escape of a nervous piggy involves holding his body from underneath, with your hand just behind the front legs. Place your index finger between your Guinea pig's front legs. This way, you can press your index finger against your Guinea pig's chest to prevent him from moving forward, or you can grasp one of his front legs in a scissor hold between your index finger and middle finger to get a firmer grip on him. This one-hand hold makes it easy to pet your Guinea pig without worrying that he will jump out of your arms.

As your Guinea pig becomes comfortable with handling, he will become much more relaxed at your touch. You'll begin to discover where your Guinea pig likes to be petted or scratched. Some Guinea pigs like to be stroked on the face; some like to be scratched on the neck or chin. Some Guinea pigs learn to enjoy handling so much that they will sit calmly in their owner's lap and purr.

Putting Down Your Pet: When you try to replace your Guinea pig in his pen, your Guinea pig will probably attempt to leap prematurely from your hand. In order to prevent injury to the Guinea pig or to you, you can keep your Guinea pig from doing this by putting him into his pen rear-first. Another method is to place one hand in front of his face to keep him from jumping out of your grasp.

When defining the rules and limits of pet handling to children, a positive approach is the most productive. Instead of telling a child what *not* to do, tell a child what to do.

ESTABLISHING RULES

Older children who have demonstrated responsible behavior can be taught how to hold and pet your Guinea pig, too. Younger children can be involved in Guinea pig handling with your assistance. Children should be taught to hold the Guinea pig with two hands—one hand around the body, and one hand over the top of the body. There should also be household rules as to when, how often, and under what circumstances children can play with your pet. This will help avoid stressing or exhausting the animal.

Along with rules and guidelines concerning handling, you should determine who will be responsible for your Guinea pig's care. Who will feed him? Who will clean his cage? And who will back these people up when they are unable to do their duties? Setting clear limits and having specific expectations will ensure that your precious piggy does not become mishandled or neglected.

INTRODUCING OTHER PETS

Setting clear limits also applies to other pets. Cats and dogs should not be allowed to harass your helplessly confined Guinea pig. Prey animals can literally become frightened to death; the fear and shock of being pursued by a large predator can cause them to suffer cardiac arrest.

When you first bring your Guinea pig home, it is ideal if you can keep him within sight and smell of your other pets so all the animals can become accustomed to each other's presence. Door gates are wonderful for keeping dogs at a safe distance while still allowing them to see, smell, and hear your Guinea pig.

Provided your dog or cat reacts favorably at a distance, you can gradually bring your pets closer together.

Introduce your Guinea pig to your other pets gradually, so that they become accustomed to each other.

FAST FACT

Can a dog and a Guinea pig become friends? It does happen, but rarely. A dog that seems to enjoy the company of a Guinea pig may suddenly launch an attack on his newfound friend when his prey drive is accidentally aroused by the Guinea pig's quick movements. Never leave a Guinea pig within unprotected reach of a dog!

Never leave dogs or cats unattended in the same room with your caged Guinea pig unless it is obvious that they get along. Ideally, this means they will pay very little attention to each other.

When all the animals have settled down and seem to tolerate each other as housemates, you can consider allowing your gentle dog or cat to sniff your Guinea pig while you are holding him. Use discretion in this, as nobody knows your pets better than you do. Always be prepared to defend your Guinea pig, as he is always the one who will bear the brunt of any conflict!

Preparing for your Guinea pig helps to lessen the stress on your new pet, but it also eases the stress on you. Bringing an animal family member into your household is an adjustment for everyone (and every animal) in your home, so it should be a priority to make this transition go smoothly. The sooner everyone gets comfortable with your new family member, the sooner you can appreciate the real joys of Guinea pig ownership!

CHAPTER FIVE

Nutrition, Exercise, Grooming, and Training

There's nothing as musical as the whistling of a happy, healthy Guinea pig! To keep your Guinea pig "singing," you need to take proper care of him. Providing nutrition, exercise, and grooming aren't just chores—they involve interacting with your pet, which means they are bonding opportunities. So take full advantage of your pet care duties to enjoy your pet!

Before you know it, your Guinea pig will be squealing in delight when you approach at feeding time. He'll

To keep your Guinea pig happy, you'll have to feed him the right foods, make sure he gets daily exercise, and keep his coat and nails trimmed to the proper length.

be nestling quietly in your lap for brushing. And he'll be begging impatiently at his cage door to come out and play when he knows it's time for exercise. Your Guinea pig learns to love you and trust you through these activities, especially if you provide them on a regular schedule.

NUTRITION

Every species of animal has its own dietary requirements. In the Guinea pig's case, there are three nutritional elements your piggy must have: commercial pellets, fresh vegetation, and roughage. Each one of these meets specific nutritional needs for your pet.

COMMERCIAL FEED: Commercially manufactured feed pellets are crucial to your Guinea pig's diet because they contain balanced dietary components. It can be difficult to provide the right vitamins in the right proportions by feeding your Guinea pig strictly fresh greens and roughage. Most important, Guinea pigs are unable to manufacture their own vitamin C, so commercial Guinea pig feed pellets are purposely fortified with this vitamin to meet this need. It is important not to substitute feed pellets made for other small animals; they may not contain the right ingredients or ingredients in the proper balance.

Dry pellets may seem to have a long shelf life, but they don't. They can become stale and moldy, just like any other type of food. Keep your pet's food fresh by storing it in an airtight container or in the refrigerator. Check the manufacture date on the package when you buy it, and don't buy more than you will use within a month's time—no matter how great a deal you can get by purchasing bulk quantities!

A young cavy can be allowed an endless supply of pellets by keeping his food dish full, but if you have an adult cavy, you will need to monitor his weight to see if you should continue this practice. Adult Guinea pigs that receive plenty of exercise (especially those that have at least one Guinea pig companion to play with) will rarely gain too much weight by free-feeding pellets. But if

While Guinea pigs definitely express their food preferences, they are not known as fussy eaters (especially when it comes to fresh foods). If your Guinea pig seems to be off his feed, it may be a sign of illness or dental problems, so have him checked out by your veterinarian.

your adult Guinea pig seems to be getting on the chunky side, which is evident by a rounded barrel shape to his body and excess body fat, you may need to limit his consumption of pellets to two tablespoons (30 ml) fed twice per day.

Your Guinea pig will appreciate fresh fruit as an occasional treat. However, limit the amount of fruit he eats. Too much will cause digestive problems.

FRESH VEGETATION: Fresh vegetation is your Guinea pig's favorite fare. You'll quickly notice that your pet reacts to it the same way a child reacts to candy. For the same reason that you would restrict a child's candy intake, you should also limit your Guinea pig's consumption of fresh vegetation—because too much isn't good for him. If your piggy eats too many fresh greens, he won't be eating enough commercial pellets to get the other vitamins and minerals he needs, and he won't be eating enough hay to get the roughage necessary for good digestion. Fresh plant material is a very important component of your Guinea pig's diet, but it should not exceed about 15 percent of his total food intake.

It can be easy to supply your pet with this portion of his diet by simply saving fresh vegetable cuttings from the preparation of your own meals. You can also buy a few extra items your Guinea pig finds particularly delectable. Guinea pigs love

Because Guinea pigs are unable to manufacture their own vitamin C, it must be provided in their diet. The following foods are good sources of vitamin C: apples, asparagus, broccoli, carrots, cauliflower, cucumber, grapes, green peppers, kiwi, oranges, peaches, peas, spinach, squash, strawberries, and tomatoes.

Vegetables and freshly cut greens make a nice supplement for your Guinea pig's commercial food pellets.

carrots, celery, bell peppers, spinach, broccoli, and romaine lettuce. Fruits like apples, grapes, and pears are held in high esteem, but they should be fed in moderation to avoid giving your pet diarrhea. Avoid items with extremely high water content, like iceberg lettuce and watermelon, for the same reason.

Always be sure to wash store-bought produce before feeding it to your pet, as pesticide and fertilizer residue could make him sick. Better yet, stick to the organic section of the grocery store. The fresh food you give your pet should be just that—fresh. A Guinea pig should not be used as a garbage disposal to clean the fridge of old, moldy, or withered vegetables. If a food is not safe for you to eat, it probably is not safe for your Guinea pig, either!

You might find some fresh food right outside your own front door. Guinea pigs love fresh grass, dandelions, and clover. A few handfuls of freshly picked greens will have your piggy purring like a motor. Again, be sure to avoid picking your pet's greens where pesticides, fertilizers, and chemicals have been sprayed, and always remove food that your Guinea pig leaves uneaten. Once picked, plants tend to decompose quickly, and this chemical process can make plant material toxic.

If you are really ambitious, you can even grow your own Guinea pig food! Coltsfoot, dead-nettles, shepherd's purse, yarrow, and Bermuda grass are all good choices for your Guinea pig's garden. Or you can share some of the fresh food from your own garden, such as tomatoes, strawberries, beet tops, melons, and green beans. If you like the idea of providing fresh-grown food for your Guinea pig but you don't want all the fuss, you can purchase pet grass kits at some pet supply stores.

Roughage: Roughage is usually provided in the form of hay. You might think hay all looks the same—like dried and bundled grass—but it's not. There are different types of grasses and plants that are dried and baled, depending on what type of animal is expected to eat it. For Guinea pigs, timothy or oat hay is the best. A timothy and alfalfa mix is acceptable, as long as the alfalfa content is not too high. Alfalfa is a very rich feed that can make your Guinea pig paunchy.

You can find hay at livestock feed stores and some pet supply stores.

POISONOUS PLANTS

Just because your Guinea pig is an herbivore does not mean he can eat any plant material. The following common plants are toxic to your pet and should be kept out of his reach:

- any bulb plants
- azalea
- bluebell
- belladonna
- buttercup
- chrysanthemum
- clematis
- columbine
- daffodil
- dahlia
- foxglove
- holly
- mistletoe
- monkshood
- oleander
- poinsettia
- ragwort
- rhododendron
- rhubarb
- St. John's wort
- wisteria
- yew

You might also be able to purchase a single bale from a local horse stable, as horse hay is usually suitable for Guinea pigs, too. Hay can be stored for at least a year, and one bale should be more than enough to last a Guinea pig for that amount of time.

Purchase hay that is dry (not wet or damp) and dust-free. If you smell the hay, it should smell sweet and grassy, not like mildew. If you slap the hay bale, there should not be clouds of dust or mold spores billowing out of it. Store your hay in a cool, dry place, and cover the top of it to keep it from getting dusty. Ideally, air should be able to circulate around the bale to prevent the condensation of moisture and the formation of mold. A fresh handful of hay per day will keep your Guinea pig munching merrily.

FAST FACT

Guinea pigs like grain as much as the mice in a barn! Horse grain, when fed in moderation, is a nice treat for your pet, but since it is usually sold in a minimum quantity of fifty-pound (23 kg) bags, you are best off finding an equestrian friend who will sell you a few scoops at a time—horse grain will get old and moldy if it is kept too long.

AT FEEDING TIME...

- ✔ Provide fresh water daily.
- ✔ Discard old food and provide fresh food daily.
- ✔ Feed your pet on a regular schedule.
- ✔ Measure food and adjust the amount according to your pet's weight.
- ✔ Offer treats sparingly.
- ✔ Introduce new foods gradually.
- ✔ Wash food and water containers at least once a week.

CECOTROPES AND COPROPHAGY

There is one essential diet component you need not worry about providing; your Guinea pig will take care of it himself. It involves the consumption of cecotropes, which are waste pellets your Guinea pig's body produces. These pellets are generally smaller and softer than normal Guinea pig waste pellets.

When an animal consumes his own waste, it is called coprophagy. This may seem disgusting to humans, but coprophagy in Guinea pigs is nature's way of providing certain nutrients that your pet cannot obtain in other ways. Realistically, you may never

FAST FACT

A Guinea pig is in good condition when his body feels firm and compact. If your piggy is looking a little too barrel-like and feels soft and squishy, limit his intake of commercial feed, avoid high-sugar fruits for a while, and cut back on treats until your little guy trims down.

even be aware that your Guinea pig is doing this, as the cecotropes are usually consumed as soon as they are expelled from the anus.

EXERCISE

Proper nutrition is only part of the equation when it comes to keeping your Guinea pig healthy and fit. Like many other pets, Guinea pigs can become obese if they eat too much and do not get enough exercise. Playtime outside of his cage is a great way to stimulate your Guinea pig's mind and body. (See chapter 7 for tips on how to provide a safe indoor or outdoor play area for your pet.)

If you are unable to provide playtime outside the cage on a daily basis, you should at least provide a cage large enough for your pet to get the exercise he needs. A cage with room to run and multiple levels can allow your pet to stretch his legs.

Environmental enrichment is also a good way to keep your piggy moving. You can put hay in different corners or on different levels in his cage, which will require him to move about in search of it. Give him large cardboard tubes to play in or tissue boxes to explore. Make him hunt for chew toys you've hidden around his cage. Of course, the best enrichment and exercise you can give your Guinea pig is a Guinea pig friend! Guinea pigs love to play and interact with each other.

GROOMING

When you think of grooming, you probably think of combing or brushing, but grooming actually encompasses all the hygiene practices necessary to keep your Guinea pig healthy. Besides hair care, this includes nail clipping, eye care, and dental care. Attending to these different body parts does more than keep your pet in top shape; it also makes your Guinea pig more tolerant of handling. So groom your pet often!

Brushing and Combing: Guinea pigs come in both short-haired and long-haired varieties, and each one has its own special care requirements. If you have a short-haired Guinea pig, hair care is not very demanding. Combing lightly with a

Your Guinea pig will appreciate an opportunity to scamper around your backyard each day, and the exercise will help keep him healthy. However, never let your piggy play unsupervised; you don't want him to get lost, or wind up becoming a meal for a larger animal!

flea comb or brushing with a soft-bristled pet brush once a week is enough to stimulate the skin and distribute natural oils throughout your Guinea pig's coat.

Use this opportunity to check your pet's coat for flaky skin, bald or thin spots, or parasites like fleas or lice. If you lay your finger flat against your Guinea pig's body and draw it against the lay of the hair, you can get a good peek at your pet's skin condition and the hair shafts.

Long-haired Guinea pigs obviously require more maintenance. You should use a slicker brush or a pin brush to detangle your long-haired Guinea pig's coat every day. You can minimize discomfort to your pet by detangling the ends of the hair first and working your way gradually toward the skin. Hold the hair close to the skin with one hand, and brush with the other hand. This will help you avoid pulling against your pet's skin.

Because grooming is more intensive for long-haired Guinea pigs, it is very important to begin grooming your long-haired Guinea pig when he is young, so he can become accustomed to this routine at a young age. If you do not plan to show your long-haired Guinea pig, it might be more practical to keep his hair trimmed to a shorter length for ease of maintenance.

HAIR TRIMMING: Trimming with blunt-tipped scissors is the safest way to crop your little guy. You can find this type of scissors where pet grooming supplies are sold. Pay particular attention to trimming your pet's rear end, as this is usually the most troublesome area when it comes to stains and soiling.

You can cut the hair back to just about any length you want, but be careful not to nick your pet's ears or toes. Guinea pigs can jerk and thrash when they are unhappy about being held, so it's best to accustom your piggy to frequent and thorough handling before attempting to trim him. To help him feel more secure, you can trim him while holding him in your lap. Keeping a towel spread across your legs beforehand will make cleanup easy, as you can simply roll the hair up in the towel and then shake it over the garbage can.

Don't worry that you are making your Guinea pig look funny—he doesn't care how he looks. He'll probably enjoy feeling cooler and cleaner. Besides, the beauty of hair is that it grows back!

BATHING: Many Guinea pigs, especially short-haired ones, rarely require a bath. But bathing is still a necessary chore for show cavies, or to clean up a pet that has gotten soiled. Like most animals, Guinea pigs are not fond of baths, so this process should be kept as brief as possible. In order to make bath time less stressful, you should have all your supplies assembled ahead of time. You'll need shampoo, conditioner (for long-haired Guinea pigs), a towel for drying, and a rubber sink mat or towel to keep your pet's feet out of the drain.

FAST FACT

The body hair of longhaired cavies never stops growing. Don't worry if you were overzealous in trimming your long-haired cavy—his hair will grow back!

Animals tend to be more comfortable being sprayed than dunked, so a spray nozzle is a good investment. Always choose the mildest pet shampoo you can find (preferably a "tearless" product, but still be careful to avoid getting suds near your pet's eyes). Keep one hand on your Guinea pig at all times so he stays safe, and wash him with the other hand. You should test the water to make sure it is not too hot or too cold. When the bath is finished, it is important to rinse your pet thoroughly. Shampoo and excess conditioner left in your pet's coat can dry out his skin or make his coat dull.

Short-haired Guinea pigs can usually be left to air dry, but you may need to give your long-haired Guinea pig a bit of help to dry off. A hair dryer will probably scare your piggy half to death, but you can still help him dry off by keeping him moving. Play with him or give him a large area to move around in, and brush the damp hair out every so often to separate the hairs.

Show Grooming: Show grooming is an art best learned by consulting with and observing those with experience. Specialized products for shampooing, conditioning, and stain

A spray attachment for your bathtub, shower, or sink will help you to gently wash your Guinea pig, as well as to rinse shampoo and grime out of his hair.

removal are often used. Tricks of the trade include bathing your show cavy several days prior to a show, so the natural oils in your Guinea pig's coat have time to replenish. These oils give your pet's coat the lustrous shine he needs to look his best!

Long-haired Guinea pigs require a beauty regimen that consists of daily brushing, regular baths, and hair wrapping. When done right, dividing the hair into sections and wrapping each section tightly in paper towels or small pieces of cloth is a skill that can preserve the quality of a Guinea pig's coat. When done wrong, it can result in dreaded tangles and hair breakage. The best way to learn how to do it right is to contact your local cavy club and find a mentor who can teach you.

You'll want to have plenty of paper towels on hand before giving your Guinea pig a bath. You'll need to make sure that he's fully dry before allowing him outside or exposing him to drafts. Otherwise, your Guinea pig could become sick.

NAIL TRIMMING: Show cavies and pet cavies both need a pedicure occasionally. Guinea pigs' nails grow continuously, and domestic Guinea pigs do not have the opportunity to wear their nails down naturally, as wild cavies do. Overgrown nails can cause painful foot problems for your pet, so you should check the length of your Guinea pig's nails frequently.

A human toenail clipper is usually sufficient to clip your pet's nails. However, if your Guinea pig has fairly large nails, you may need to purchase a small pet nail clipper. This job might seem intimidating at first, but confidence can only be gained through practice. The same thing goes for your Guinea pig—he may not be comfortable with this procedure at first, but frequent handling of his feet and regular nail trims will teach him to tolerate it.

Cuddle your Guinea pig in your lap and check each of his

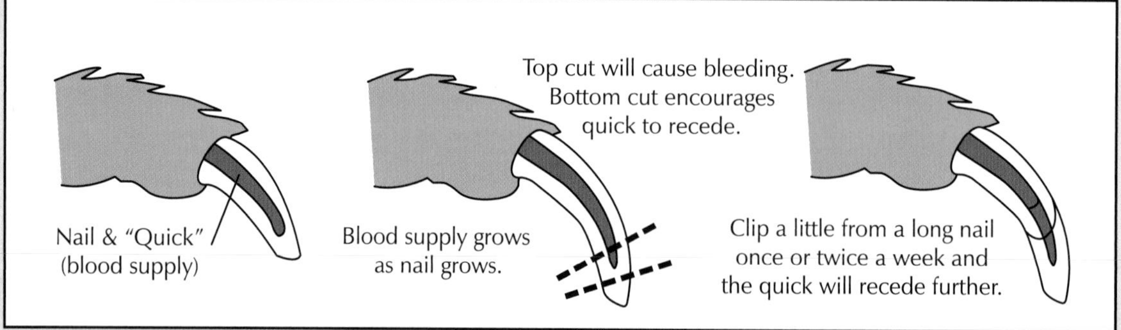
Top cut will cause bleeding.
Bottom cut encourages
quick to recede.
Nail & "Quick"
(blood supply)
Blood supply grows
as nail grows.
Clip a little from a long nail
once or twice a week and
the quick will recede further.

Be careful when trimming your Guinea pig's nails. As the illustration above shows, if you regularly clip the nail close to the quick without nicking it, over time the quick will recede within the nail. This will allow you to trim your Guinea pig's nails even shorter.

feet. When trimming his nails, cut off only the tip. If your Guinea pig has white nails, you can see the dark "quick" inside the nail, which provides the nail's blood supply. As long as you do not cut into the quick, you will not hurt your pet. If your Guinea pig has dark nails, you will have to estimate where the quick is by observing the length and the tapering of the nail. It's better to leave the nails a little too long than to cut them too short and risk injuring your little guy.

If you do cut the quick, the nail will bleed for a short time. If you have a styptic pencil, you can dab it on the end of the nail to help stop the bleeding. Corn starch will also help clot the blood and stop the nail from bleeding.

After you're finished trimming your Guinea pig's nails, it's a good idea to give him a treat. This will teach your Guinea pig that he'll be rewarded each time his nails are trimmed.

HEALTH CHECK: Grooming provides an excellent opportunity to perform a health check on your pet. Most health problems have a much better prognosis when they are diagnosed early, so be observant about your Guinea pig's attitude and general appearance. If he seems sluggish or his coat looks dull or unkempt, he may need veterinary attention. Discharge from his nose or eyes, difficulty breathing, limping, or other signs of physical injury—these are indications that your Guinea pig needs medical attention.

Your grooming routine should include a check of your Guinea pig's eyes, because it's very common for

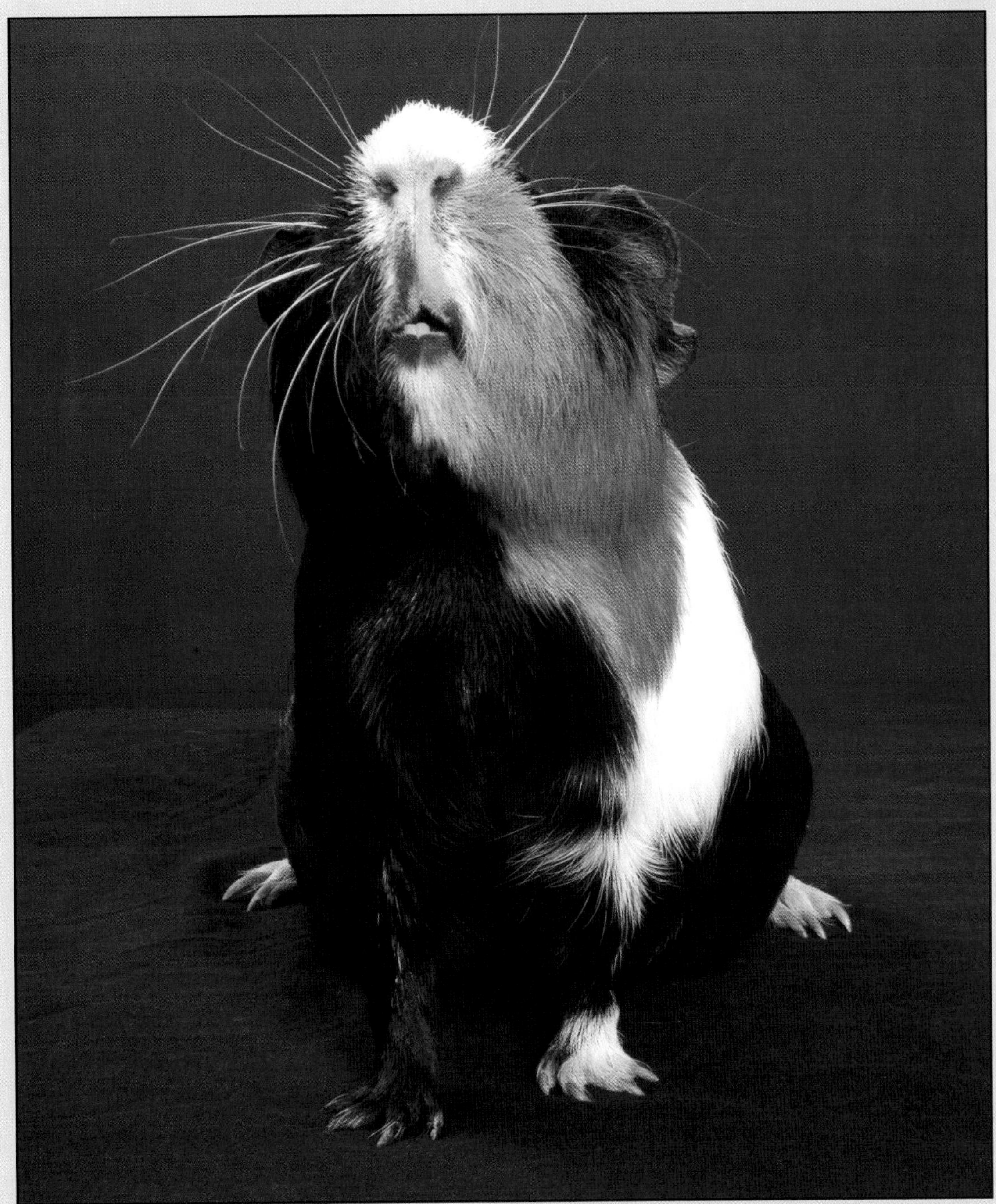

Guinea pigs have incisor teeth at the front of their mouths—two incisors on the top and two on the bottom. You should check these teeth regularly. Make sure no teeth are broken. Teeth that are slanted indicate irregular wear. Broken teeth will grow back, although you may want to take your Guinea pig to a veterinarian or animal dentist to have him checked.

Guinea pigs to get slivers of hay or bedding material in their eyes. If you see any debris in your pet's eyes, remove it carefully by working it toward the corner of the eye where you can get hold of it and pull it out. When your pet's eye has been irritated, it may develop a cloudy, filmlike appearance—this is a part of the normal healing process and it should clear up within a week or two.

Your Guinea pig's incisor teeth can also cause problems for him if they become overgrown. Provide plenty of chewing material for your Guinea pig and check his mouth frequently. Signs of overgrown teeth or other dental problems include mouth sores, lack of appetite, and weight loss. Consult your veterinarian about any dental problems.

LITTER BOX TRAINING

Many people are surprised to find out that Guinea pigs can be litter box trained. This training is especially desirable if you plan to allow your Guinea pig to roam the floor. Thanks to litter box training, some Guinea pigs have become true house pets with free access to any room in the house. Whether or not your Guinea pig is a candidate for "free roaming" depends on his personality, if he has any destructive tendencies, if there are other pets or small children in the house, and what precautions can be taken to keep him safe. But even if your Guinea pig is not free-roaming material, litter box training can still come in handy for those short playtimes outside the cage.

There are two important things to realize about litter box training a Guinea pig. First, Guinea pigs cannot be expected to use a litter box 100 percent of the time. In general, they are not as reliable as cats or rabbits. And second, not all Guinea pigs are receptive to litter box training. You can tap into your pet's natural preference to defecate in a certain area, but this preference can sometimes be usurped by convenience or opportunity. In other words, you must be willing to forgive a misplaced pellet here and there!

To begin this training, you need to have enough room in your Guinea pig's cage for a small litter box. You can use any low-sided plastic box, but it must have a doorway in the side of it to make it easy for your pet to get in and out of it. Your sensitive Guinea pig will prefer an unscented, dust-free type of litter material. Put the litter box in an area of the cage where your Guinea pig has already shown a preference to defecate. Place a few of his pellets in the litter box; this will help him understand what you want him to do there.

When your Guinea pig appears to be using his litter box consistently in his cage, you can offer it to him on the floor. Always put the box in the same place so your Guinea pig knows where to find it. (See chapter 7 to learn how clicker training can help your Guinea pig get the right idea.)

❧❧❧

Taking care of your Guinea pig's needs helps you develop a close relationship with your pet. It makes your Guinea pig feel good. When a Guinea pig feels good, it shows in his bright eyes, shiny coat, and upbeat attitude. Guinea pig ownership isn't just about having a Guinea pig for a friend; it's also about being a good friend to your Guinea pig!

CHAPTER SIX

Health Issues Your Guinea Pig May Face

Guinea pigs are a hardy lot; that's one of the reasons they have become such popular pets. But this doesn't mean that Guinea pigs never get sick or never require veterinary care. Even though serious health problems are rare in Guinea pigs, this species is rather short-lived, so it is in your and your pet's best interest to do everything you

If you want to keep your Guinea pig happy, be alert to possible health issues. Guinea pigs are a hardy species, but they are susceptible to certain physical problems.

can to maximize your Guinea pig's time on this earth.

CHOOSING A GUINEA PIG VETERINARIAN

The first step to ensuring your Guinea pig's health and well-being is to find a veterinarian. This task is not quite as simple as some people think, as not all veterinarians are experts in cavies. There are so many different species of animals that it's impossible to find a veterinarian who is knowledgeable and experienced with them all. Treatments for one species can be deadly for another, so it's very important to choose a veterinarian who has specific training and expertise in Guinea pigs.

Veterinarians who specialize in so-called "exotic pets" have received additional instruction in the health requirements and treatment of Guinea pigs, as well as other rare or unusual pets. You can locate a veterinarian with this specialty by asking your pet's breeder or other Guinea pig owners, researching veterinarians in the phone book, checking with your local cavy club, or checking the member directory of the Association of Exotic Mammal Veterinarians (AEMV) at www.aemv.org. Finding a specialized vet can mean the difference between solving a health problem the first time around or going through a frustrating trial-and-error period to get the correct diagnosis and treatment.

Locating a vet with the right specialty is only one of the criteria in choosing a vet. You also need to consider location, price, and emergency care. A veterinarian won't do you much good if she's inaccessible to you because of distance or limited office hours. So find a vet who is located as close to your home as possible, and make sure her hours won't conflict with your work schedule.

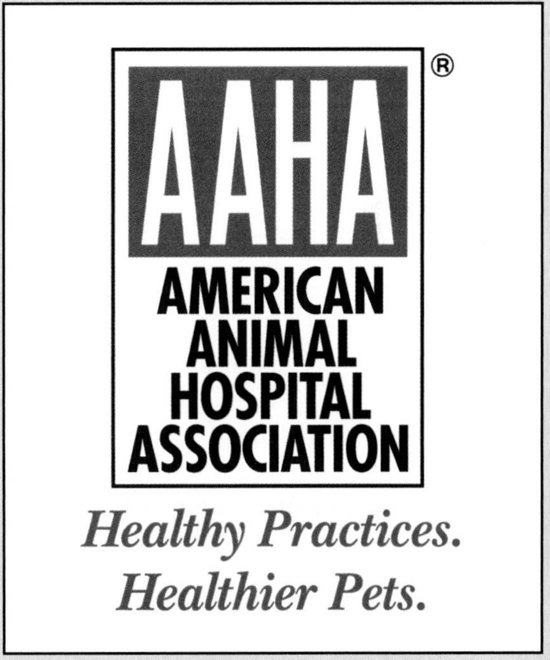

Ideally, a prospective veterinary clinic should be a member of the American Animal Hospital Association or a similar organization that inspects and accredits veterinary facilities.

The veterinary profession is a competitive field, so it doesn't hurt to compare prices, especially for routine care. But keep in mind that there are occasions when you get what you pay for. Veterinary clinics that boast the latest in equipment, have extended emergency hours, or provide their own laboratory services are likely to charge a little more. Always keep prices in perspective when deciding how much you're willing to pay.

Gone are the days when veterinarians made house calls (although a few still do this) or provided round-the-clock services, so you should keep information on the nearest twenty-four-hour emergency vet clinic handy. Placing your veterinarian's phone number on your fridge, or some other place where you list emergency phone numbers, can save you valuable time when you need it the most.

When you have found a veterinarian who meets your expectations, plan a visit to the hospital or clinic to get a feel for the overall organization of the facility. Do staff members treat both humans and animals with courtesy and respect? Do they seem organized and efficient? Are the rooms clean and well-maintained? Most important, do you feel comfortable with the veterinarian? If the answer is "yes" to all these questions, you have found your match!

FAST FACT

Many veterinarians are now specializing in alternative therapies that include acupuncture, homeopathy, herbal medicine, and chiropractic care, among others. Holistic therapies are often used in conjunction with conventional medicine. If you think your Guinea pig might benefit from an alternative therapy, check the Web site of the American Holistic Veterinary Medical Association (AHVMA) at www.ahvma.org to find a holistic veterinarian in your area.

THE FIRST VETERINARY EXAM

Even though Guinea pigs are not required to have vaccinations like dogs and cats, it is still important for them to have annual physical exams. Your vet may be able to detect signs of illness that have escaped your untrained eye. Your vet may also notice weight gain that occurred so gradually you never realized it. If you have any concerns about a bald spot, a funny-looking toenail, or some strange behavior your piggy has developed, your vet will be able to answer all your questions at this time.

Your veterinarian will provide a thorough health check that includes listening to your pet's heart and lungs, examining his eyes and nose for signs of illness, checking his mouth for signs of dental problems, checking the condition of his skin and coat, and palpating his body for lumps and bumps. This kind of preventative health care can help detect problems early and improve the prognosis of many conditions.

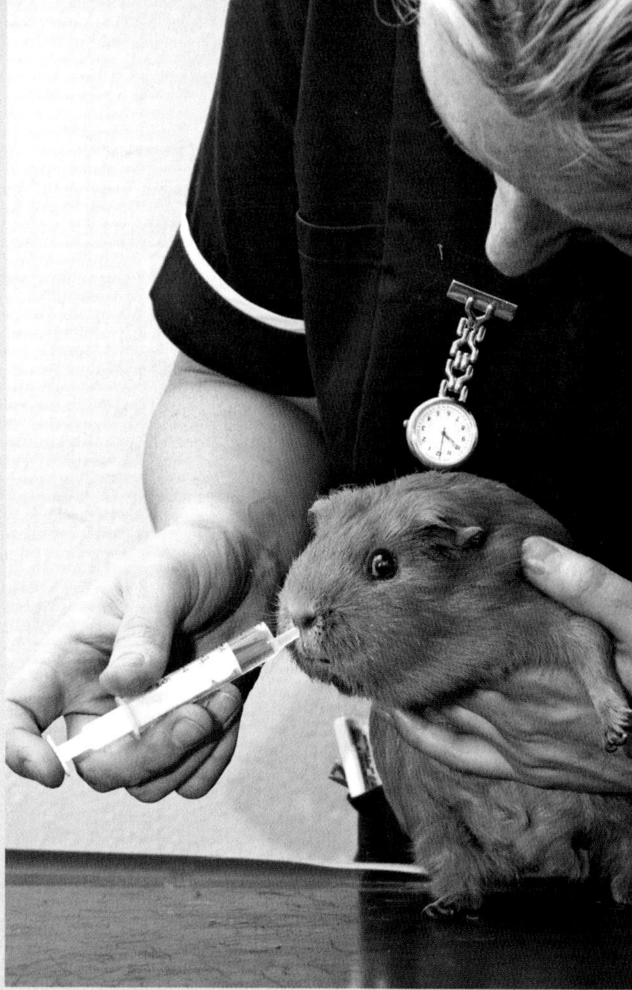

Unlike some pets, your Guinea pig won't require costly vaccinations. However, he should be thoroughly examined by a veterinarian at least once each year. This animal doctor is feeding a Guinea pig medicine through a syringe.

PARASITES

A common health condition that benefits from prompt veterinary attention is parasite infestation. Several parasites are known to target Guinea pigs, and all of them can be effectively treated with medications or topical treatments prescribed by your vet.

Lice: Lice are extremely tiny insects, but they can be seen with the naked eye. You may notice these long, thread-thin creatures crawling around the hair and skin of your Guinea pig. They'll cause your pet to scratch frequently, which may, in turn, lead to some hair loss or skin lesions.

Fortunately, Guinea pig lice are not interested in other mammals, like dogs, cats, or humans. They are easily exterminated with a couple treatments of an insecticidal product prescribed by your veterinarian. Lice are highly contagious among Guinea pigs, so take precautions to prevent them from spreading. If you have more than one Guinea pig, you'll have to treat them all and thoroughly clean and disinfect their living quarters.

MITES: Mites can cause the same itchy discomfort as lice, but you won't be able to see them. Only your veterinarian can diagnose them, by examining skin scrapings from your Guinea pig under a microscope. Symptoms to watch for include patchy hair loss and red, scabby skin. These bugs, too, can be treated with an appropriate insecticidal product prescribed by your veterinarian.

WORMS: Like other animals that feast on plant material, your Guinea pig can easily ingest the eggs of parasitic worms. Roundworms and tapeworms are common in Guinea pigs. They can have a serious impact on your pet's general health. If your Guinea pig becomes infested with parasitic worms, his skin and coat condition will appear poor, his weight and appetite may decline, and his belly may appear bloated. You may also notice roundworms or tapeworm segments in your pet's feces.

Medication to treat one type of parasitic worm may not be effective on other types of worms, so your veterinarian needs to determine which worm is the culprit and prescribe the proper medication. You can help prevent an infestation by always washing your Guinea pig's fresh greens before feeding them to your pet.

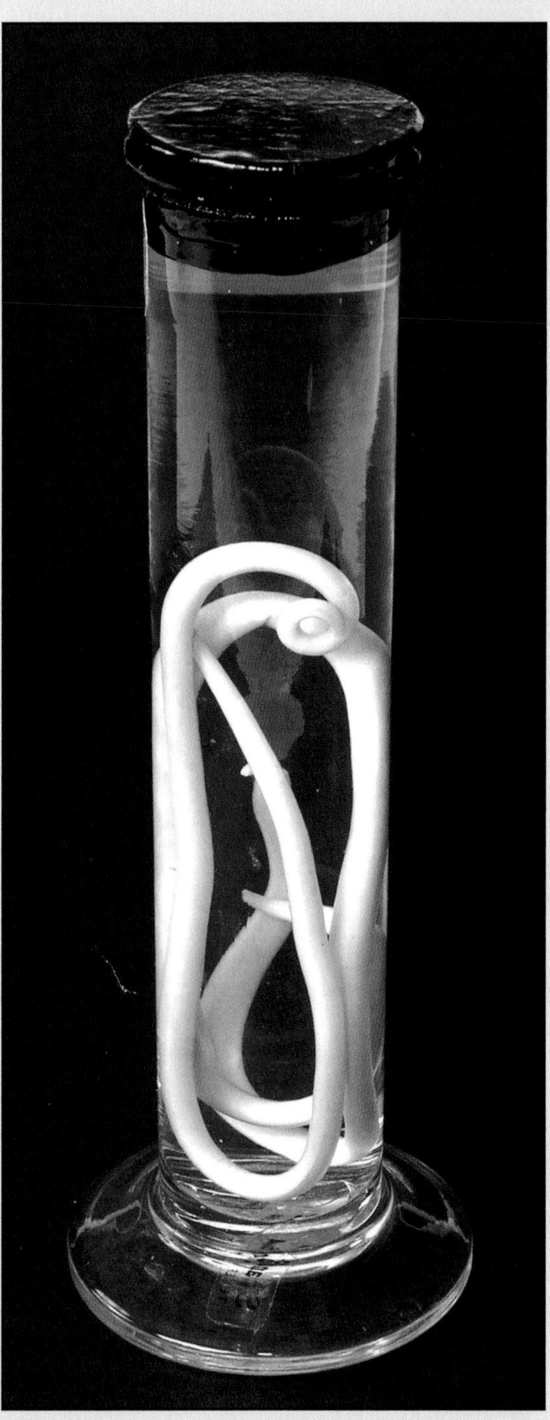

Photo of a roundworm, a common parasite that can place a strain on your Guinea pig's health.

FLEAS: Fleas are very bothersome pests that will infect other pets in your home as well as your Guinea pig. These dark-colored insects can easily be seen scurrying along your pet's skin. They also leave behind tiny black flecks of waste, called "flea dirt," that indicate their presence. Be aware that getting rid of your pets will not get rid of the fleas. Without a furry creature to target, fleas will simply begin to bite people!

Fleas are usually brought into your home from the outside, so if your Guinea pig is kept indoors, he is probably not the source of the flea infestation. All the pets in your home will need to be treated, so you should consult your veterinarian to find out what type of flea treatment to use for each species. Indoor and outdoor areas will also need to be treated, as fleas will lay their eggs anywhere your pets spend their time. Several treatments of both your pets and their environment are usually required to eradicate fleas, because flea eggs that have not hatched yet are impervious to insecticides.

Fleas are more than just irritating pests. Some fleas carry diseases that can be harmful to your Guinea pig.

FAST FACT

A Guinea pig that spends time outdoors, in a hutch or play area, has greater exposure to parasites like intestinal worms and fleas. If you leave your Guinea pig outside for any amount of time, check him for symptoms frequently, so parasite infestations can be addressed early.

COMMON HEALTH CONDITIONS

There are several common health conditions that plague the Guinea pig species, most of which can be avoided with proper care. You should be familiar with their symptoms and treatment so that their ill effects can be minimized in case they occur.

SCURVY: Guinea pigs cannot manufacture their own vitamin C, which makes them particularly prone to

FAST FACT

Guinea pigs are not particularly fond of taking medications. This task can be accomplished more easily if you wrap your Guinea pig in a towel first. This will help your piggy feel safer, while also preventing him from wriggling away from you.

vitamin C deficiency. This vitamin must be provided in adequate amounts in your Guinea pig's diet, or he may begin to show symptoms of scurvy, including swollen and painful joints, poor appetite, lethargy, and bleeding gums. This condition can be fatal, so veterinary treatment is imperative. A diet adjustment will be necessary to avoid a recurrence.

Heat Prostration: Guinea pigs are prone to heat prostration, because they do not have much tolerance for hot temperatures. This becomes a problem when they are left outside in hutches. You can tell that your Guinea pig is becoming overheated when he stretches his body out in an effort to cool off. His breathing may become rapid or he may begin panting. If this happens, you must cool him off as quickly as possible by putting a cold, wet towel around him. Heat prostration can be serious, so have your overheated pet checked out by your veterinarian.

Obesity: Some Guinea pigs have a tendency to get a little chunky in the middle. This isn't surprising, since grazing animals like Guinea pigs are genetically programmed to eat constantly. You can prevent this problem by monitoring your pet's weight and restricting his food intake. In particular, cut back on the commercial pellets you are feeding him and limit fruits and treats. It is better to give him a little more roughage (hay) and a little less of these higher-calorie items.

Realistically, a trifle of extra weight doesn't do much harm to a Guinea pig, especially if he appears to be happy and healthy. Just make sure your pet gets some exercise and has some diversions, like chewing

FAST FACT

Some conditions, like mange (caused by sarcoptic mites) or ringworm (caused by a fungus), can be spread to other pets. Be sure to isolate your sick Guinea pig from your other household pets.

Chewing things—even the side of his hide box—will help keep your Guinea pig's teeth the proper length.

blocks, so eating isn't the only thing he has to do!

MALOCCLUSION: One of the few genetic problems that affect Guinea pigs is when the top incisor teeth do not overlap the bottom incisor teeth properly. This is called malocclusion, and it can affect your Guinea pig's health if he is unable to eat properly. Weight loss and loss of appetite, mouth sores, and wetness of the chin are all signs of teeth problems. Adequate trimming or filing of the teeth may allow the Guinea pig with misaligned teeth to eat. Your veterinarian can assist you with this, or she can teach you how to do it yourself.

RESPIRATORY INFECTIONS: Respiratory infections can be caused by either a virus or a bacterium. Symptoms may include sneezing, discharge from the eyes or nose, lethargy, and loss of appetite. Bacterial infections can be treated with antibiotics, while viral infections can only be treated with supportive care to minimize the symptoms. Your veterinarian will have to determine the cause and necessary treatment. To prevent respiratory infections, make sure the hay you feed your pet is not damp, moldy, or dusty, and keep your pet's cage away from drafts.

Fungal Infections: Ringworm is not caused by a worm at all. It is a fungal infection that got its name from its circular pattern of infection. Although ringworm is rare in Guinea pigs, environment and stress can contribute to its development. It usually begins on the face and develops into circular, scaly, crusty patches of skin. Once established, it is contagious, so precautions should be taken to prevent its spread.

Ringworm can spread to other Guinea pigs or other pets. Although most adult humans are resistant to it, children may be susceptible, so handling of the infected Guinea pig by children should be halted until the infection is brought under control.

When you hold your Guinea pig, be alert to signs of trouble around his eyes. They should be bright and clear, as in the photo above. A discharge of fluid from around the eye is a sign that something is wrong.

Your veterinarian can prescribe the appropriate topical treatment, and anything that the fungal spores can potentially penetrate should be discarded. This includes wooden or cardboard nest boxes and playthings.

Ear Infections: Ear infections do not occur very often, but when they do, they can cause plenty of discomfort for your Guinea pig. Symptoms include head shaking and ear scratching. A more serious case will cause the Guinea pig to carry his head in a tilted position. See your veterinarian for treatment, as antibiotics may be necessary to treat the condition.

Fatty Eye: A condition that often affects older boars is called fatty eye. This condition is characterized by a swelling of the lower eye muscle, and it looks as if the eye has been irritated by a foreign body. It can affect one or both eyes, but it is not considered a problem. There is no known cure for it, but it does not seem to cause any discomfort or loss of vision for the Guinea pig.

Cataracts: The Guinea pig is prone to cataracts, just like many other mammals. This condition can be hereditary, so Guinea pigs with this condition should not be bred. Cataracts can result in partial or total blindness. Because surgery to remove cataracts is quite expensive and blind cavies do not experience much difficulty getting around in their limited, caged environments, the condition is usually not surgically corrected for this species.

Diarrhea: Diarrhea in the Guinea pig can be caused by a number of conditions and illnesses. Most of the time, however, it is an indication of inappropriate diet. Spoiled or rotten food can cause diarrhea, as can too much of certain foods like iceberg lettuce. This problem can be remedied by adjusting your pet's diet. Reduce the problem-causing food and increase your pet's roughage.

If a diet change doesn't resolve the problem, or your pet displays other symptoms, a trip to your veterinarian is called for. Don't let this

FAST FACT

You should only use medications, dips, medicated shampoos, and even herbal remedies that are specifically formulated for Guinea pigs. Treatments that may be effective for another species may be deadly for Guinea pigs.

problem persist very long, as it takes very little time for such a small animal to become dehydrated!

Constipation: Constipation is characterized by waste pellets that appear smaller and drier than normal. If your Guinea pig receives sufficient fresh foods in his diet, constipation should not be a problem. If constipation occurs in conjunction with other symptoms, your veterinarian needs to diagnose the underlying problem.

Signs of illness or injury include the following:

- Bald spots
- Bleeding gums or mouth sores
- Bloated belly
- Constipation
- Diarrhea
- Difficulty breathing
- Dull coat or eyes
- Excessive scratching
- Head tilt
- Lack of appetite
- Lethargy
- Runny nose
- Sneezing
- Sore hocks
- Squealing (as in pain)
- Squinty or irritated eye
- Swollen joints
- Weight loss

Impacted Boars: Impaction is a condition that usually occurs with older boars. The bowel muscles become stretched with age and the Guinea pig's soft pellets (cecotropes) begin to form large lumps. It can be extremely painful for the boar to pass such large lumps, and he may indicate his discomfort by squealing. Your veterinarian may be able to show you how to help your aged boar expel these lumps, but once your pet has developed this problem, impaction will usually recur, and there is no cure for it. Severe impaction can cause extreme pain and bleeding from the anus. In this case, humane euthanasia may be the best option.

INJURIES

Guinea pigs are known to get into skirmishes with each other. They are also high-strung prey animals, and their instinct to flee can make them somewhat prone to accidents. In addition, they are curious little creatures that tend to get into things they shouldn't. As a result, Guinea pigs are subject to occasional injuries.

Abscesses: When Guinea pigs fight, their teeth are their weapons of choice. Those fanglike incisors can inflict nasty puncture wounds that can easily become infected. When they do become infected, a painful lump called an abscess develops. The abscess often has a hole in the middle where the infectious material drains out of it. Veterinary treatment may consist of lancing the abscess or prescribing antibiotics.

Fortunately, Guinea pigs do not often inflict such serious damage to each other. But if you do have Guinea pigs that fight constantly or viciously, your pets may need to be housed separately.

Sore Hocks: When Guinea pigs are housed in wire-bottom cages, it is common for them to experience soreness in their hocks, the joints of the hind legs that touch the ground when they are sitting. This problem can be resolved and prevented by providing your Guinea pig with solid flooring. Your Guinea pig should have solid flooring in at least a portion of his cage, so that he can find relief from the wire, which is painful and damaging to his soft-padded feet.

Bumblefoot: Injuries to the hocks can become infected, resulting in a condition known as bumblefoot, or pododermatitis. There will be swelling and discharge from the feet, and treatment with antibiotics may be necessary. In addition, you will need to keep your pet's cage meticulously clean in order to give his feet a chance to heal without threat of reinfection. See your vet about treating this painful condition, and again, be sure to provide solid footing for your pet.

Eye Injuries: Eye injuries can be quite common with Guinea pigs, as they are prone to getting hay seeds, grain husks, and bedding material in their eyes. A squinty, watery eye is a good indication that your Guinea pig has gotten debris in his eye. The lids may become red and inflamed, and the eye may eventually develop a cloudy appearance.

An over-the-counter antibiotic cream, such as Neosporin, can be used to treat cuts or punctures on your Guinea pig's skin. This will help to keep them from becoming infected and forming abscesses.

Providing a solid floor in your Guinea pig's cage, and covering it with newspaper or wood chips, will help prevent injuries to your piggy's feet and rear legs.

If you can remove the irritant-causing debris, do so. An eye wash can be helpful in cleaning the eye and minimizing irritation. Since minor eye injuries may occur throughout your Guinea pig's life, it's a good idea to check your pet's eyes frequently and keep them as clean as possible.

NEUTERING AND SPAYING

Having your Guinea pig surgically sterilized can be an expensive proposition and is not necessary in most situations. There may be occasions when such surgery is medically necessary, as in the case of medical conditions that affect the reproductive organs. It might be a consideration, too, if you insist on housing a male and female Guinea pig together but you don't want them to reproduce. But you do need to consider that, aside from the expense, there are potentially serious risks involved in performing surgery on small animals.

If your goal is to reduce the likelihood of fights between Guinea pigs of the same sex, the consensus is that neutering and spaying has very little effect on the natural sexual aggression of this species. The gender of your Guinea pigs and their housing arrangements are things best thought out ahead of time, and you must be prepared to house aggressive Guinea pigs separately if necessary.

If you do choose the option of neutering or spaying your Guinea pig, be prepared to provide a quiet, restricted environment for your pet so he can heal for a few days afterward. Follow your veterinarian's advice on postoperative care, and watch for signs of infection.

❧❧❧

When it comes to health conditions, prevention is always the best policy. And when health problems can't be avoided, advance preparations can mean the difference between life and death for your pet. Do you know how to recognize the signs of illness in your Guinea pig so you can address problems early? Do you know where you will take your Guinea pig when he needs emergency health care? If you can answer these questions, you are in a position to ensure the best health possible for your pet!

CHAPTER SEVEN

Enjoying Your Guinea Pig

Guinea pigs are naturally fun! They're fun to show off to your friends. They're fun to watch, especially when they're being silly. They're fun to listen to when they purr with contentment or squeal with excitement. They're fun to hold and cuddle. But, believe it or not, there are a lot of other fun things you can do with this incredible animal.

PLAYTIME

Observing your Guinea pig at play is truly entertaining, so don't forget to give your pet a new toy from time to time. You can even rotate his toys so

Guinea pigs will enjoy playing with their human friends.

he doesn't get bored with his playthings. Wood blocks to chew on, cardboard boxes to hide in, paper bags to nibble on, and cardboard tubes to go through are all things your Guinea pig will enjoy exploring and manipulating! Your Guinea pig will get even more exercise out of playtime if you take him out of his cage to play in a larger area.

Indoor Play Area: Choose a room in your house that can be made Guinea pig-proof, so you can let your pet play on the floor. Any size room is fine, but a bathroom or laundry room will probably have fewer hazards to consider. The room must have a door or a sufficient barrier to keep the Guinea pig inside the room while keeping other pets outside the room.

To make the room safe, check to make sure there are no electrical cords or other chewing hazards near floor level. Cords that cannot be removed should be covered so your Guinea pig cannot chew on them. Heating ducts at floor level should also be covered, so your pet does not fall into them. Most important, make sure your Guinea pig cannot get stuck behind or underneath appliances and furniture. These areas can be blocked off with pieces of cardboard or anything else that will help prevent your Guinea pig from getting into a tight spot.

If it is too difficult to find a suitable place in your home to allow your Guinea pig to stretch his legs, you can also use a playpen or a puppy pen as a play area (as long as the Guinea pig cannot squeeze through or gnaw through the metal or fabric mesh). You can even construct your own indoor exercise pen if you are so inclined.

Once your indoor pen is set up, you can experiment with different objects to see how your Guinea pig reacts to them. Maybe your Guinea pig thinks balls are fascinating. Maybe he is most interested in finding something to chew on. Or maybe he loves exploring new places to

When your Guinea pig roams the house, make sure he can't reach electrical outlets or cords.

hide. You can entice your Guinea pig to follow a trail of carrot "crumbs," or coax him through an obstacle course of cardboard tunnels.

Outdoor Play Area: Guinea pigs love fresh air as much as anybody else, so when the weather is nice, consider providing your little buddy with an outdoor play area. Since Guinea pigs like fresh grass even more than fresh air, ponder the possibility of providing portable five-by-five-foot (1.5m x 1.5m) fencing that can be moved to different locations in the yard. This will give your pet a constant supply of succulent greenery to munch on. It can also be moved out of the way for easy lawn mowing.

If you're all thumbs when it comes to building things, there are many collapsible outdoor cat enclosures on the market that will suit a Guinea pig just fine. Regardless of the type of enclosure you use, it must have netting or a screen over the top. There are many animals that would love to make a meal of your Guinea pig, including stray dogs, hawks, foxes, and coyotes. Make sure your outdoor pen is secure enough to keep your Guinea pig inside and other animals outside.

Your pet's outdoor pen should have plenty of shade, and a nest box should be provided to give your Guinea pig a sense of security. If your Guinea pig will be spending more than 10 or 15 minutes outside at a time, place a water bottle in the pen as well. If your outdoor space has no grass, a good pile of timothy hay to forage through will create an outdoor heaven for your little guy.

Feeding and grooming a pet Guinea pig can be a good way for children to learn about responsibility. However, an adult must always oversee what the child is doing, and make sure that the piggy receives proper care.

TRAINING

Guinea pigs have their own brand of intelligence. They can learn just about anything you'd like to teach them, as long as they are physically capable of doing it, and, most important, if what you want them to do is something they want to do!

Clicker Training: The first part of training—helping your Guinea pig understand what you want—is accomplished by "marking" the behaviors you like. Using a consistent form of communication to let your Guinea pig know when he is doing the right thing makes it easier for him to understand what you want him to do. Many trainers use clickers, which are small, handheld devices that make a distinctive clicking sound, to "mark" their Guinea pigs' behavior. A Guinea pig learns very quickly that when he hears a click, he's on the right track.

In order for this type of communication to work, you need to have impeccable timing. Always click when your Guinea pig is displaying the behavior you want. If you want to teach your Guinea pig to come to the door of his cage, click as soon as he comes to the door of his cage, not when he has been standing by the door for some time, or after he has already started to walk away. If you click too early or too late, you might end up encouraging your Guinea pig to perform a behavior you did not intend!

A wonderful source of information on clicker-training small animals is the book *Getting Started: Clicking with Your Rabbit*, by Joan Orr and Teresa Lewin. Although this book focuses on rabbits, the same techniques work just as well on Guinea pigs.

The reason the Guinea pig associates the click with a particular behavior, and the reason he wants to perform that behavior for you, is that each click should always be followed immediately by a food reward. This reward needs to be something especially delectable to your pet, like small cubes of carrots or apples. Many animals are willing to work for valuable food rewards, even Guinea pigs!

FAST FACT

Clicker training can also work without a clicker. Replace the click with a cluck, a kissing noise, or any distinctive sound that your pet can learn to associate as a marker for the right behavior.

Treats like fresh vegetables are a great way to reward your Guinea pig when he does what you want him to do.

Training Tips: Some of the things you might want to teach your Guinea pig include coming when called, going through a tunnel, or going back to his cage after playtime. You can use clicker training to help litter box train your Guinea pig. You can also use it to resolve various behavior issues. If your Guinea pig is nervous about being held or struggles when you try to trim his nails, he can be taught to tolerate these things more calmly.

Keep in mind that many behaviors need to be taught in small steps. If you want your Guinea pig to calm down when he's being handled, start out by clicking and rewarding him when he remains calm for only a second, and then terminate his handling immediately. Gradually increase the time you expect him to remain calm before clicking, rewarding, and releasing him. If you try to progress too fast, your Guinea pig may begin to have difficulty remaining calm for as long as you expect. In that case, back up a few steps and shorten the time you expect your pet to stay calm.

Any skill that your Guinea pig seems to have difficulty learning can be made easier for him by breaking it down into smaller steps. If you want to teach your piggy to go to his cage after playtime, first, place a tasty treat in his cage and click and reward him if he takes even a few steps in the right direction. Gradually increase the number of steps he must take before you click and reward him. Eventually, he will be walking all the way to his cage. When he gets to this point, you can name his behavior with a command, like "Home," so he can learn to respond to that.

Once you start experimenting with training your Guinea pig, you'll be amazed at how smart and versatile your little friend is. And if your Guinea pig's smarts surprise you, imagine how impressed your friends will be! You'll realize that you can do so much more with a Guinea pig than just holding and petting him.

SHOWING

Showing is a sport reserved for the most serious of Guinea pig enthusiasts. Maintaining a show pig and attending shows involves a definite

Showing Guinea pigs like this Silkie involves a lot of work, but you can take pride in your piggy's accomplishments!

FAST FACT

In the Guinea pig show world, a cavy is considered a "senior" when it is only six months old!

commitment of time and expense, but the rewards of showing off your fuzzy pride and joy can be enormous. This can also be quite an obsessive hobby, so plan on providing facilities for a sizable Guinea pig family!

Getting involved in showing actually begins before you acquire your first show pig. You need to study the standards for the breed of your choice so you can recognize a Guinea pig of exceptional quality. You should obtain a copy of the Standard of Perfection, a publication issued by the ARBA, which outlines the breed standards for all purebred cavies. Attending local cavy shows will give you a firsthand look at how these shows are run, and it will put you in contact with reputable breeders of show-quality cavies.

After acquiring a good show prospect, your Guinea pig will have to be registered with the ARBA. This is accomplished by becoming a member of the ARBA and having your Guinea pig inspected by an ARBA registrar. You will need to provide a three-generation pedigree for your animal. The registrar will then assign a registration number and attach a metal ear tag with this number to your Guinea pig's ear. There is a brief moment of pain during this procedure, but Guinea pigs don't appear to be any worse for wear afterward.

Some of the awards you may be eligible to win include best of breed, best of opposite sex, best of variety, and best in show. You can even earn a grand championship by acquiring three legs (wins) toward this title! You can proudly display the ribbons and trophies you earn, and sometimes cash prizes make the victories even sweeter. Best of all, you get to socialize with other people who love Guinea pigs as much as you do!

4-H: Showing can be enjoyed by children and adults alike. For children, a great place to get started is by joining a local 4-H group. Children can learn about breed standards and show rules by participating in county and state fair competitions. They can even show mixed-breed cavies in a showmanship class.

Entrants in 4-H shows do not have to be registered or ear-tagged, which is a situation that might be more acceptable to a child who wishes to show a beloved pet. The experience is undoubtedly a great way to learn more about Guinea pig care and handling.

The National 4-H Headquarters Web site, www.national4-hheadquarters.gov, provides links to the 4-H districts throughout the country. Each district Web site is different. Some include links to the local 4-H groups in that district and some do not. If not, you will have to contact the district Web site to get more information on local groups.

BREEDING

In many cases, showing leads to breeding. The challenge to produce the perfect Guinea pig is one that many Guinea pig fanciers cannot resist. It is also great fun for those with a passion for Guinea pigs. But there is one very important issue that should be considered before embarking on a piggy production venture: What is to become of your Guinea pig's offspring?

Planning how you will handle the result of your breeding efforts not only will help you avoid an uncontrollable population boom in your own home, but it will also prevent you from contributing to the greater national problem of pet overpopulation. How will you find homes for the Guinea pigs that are not destined to become part of your showing or breeding efforts?

Before breeding Guinea pigs, do some research. Certain breeds should never be permitted to mate with each other, as their offspring can have serious genetic problems.

Responsible breeders are very selective in choosing Guinea pigs with the right physical and temperamental qualities to breed. They keep detailed pedigrees and medical records on all their furry subjects. They also have specific goals for their breeding programs. Are you up to the task?

INTRODUCING THE SEXES: Population control dictates that boars and sows be kept separate until or unless you decide to allow breeding. Be aware that females should be bred before the age of ten months. After that age, their pelvic bones become fused, making it difficult and possibly fatal to go through the birthing process (a condition called "dystocia"). If a female is not bred by this age, she should never be bred.

When you are ready to introduce a male and female, they should be introduced on neutral territory. A female Guinea pig goes into season every sixteen to seventeen days, so

Breeding can be very hard on the sow (mother). When they are born, Guinea pig pups are large, covered with fur, and active. During pregnancy, the sow's weight may double, which can stress her heart and circulatory system. It has been estimated that about 20 percent of the time, the sow and pups may die due to complications during the pregnancy.

Small litters (one or two pups) can mean larger pups, which can result in birthing problems. Litters of three or four pups are better.

she should be kept with a male for at least three weeks to make sure her estrus cycle is covered sufficiently.

Pregnancy lasts for about seventy days, and birth is usually uneventful for these expertly prolific creatures. It is best to leave the business of birthing up to the female. Without interference, first pregnancies tend to produce two offspring, while subsequent litters average four offspring.

Baby Guinea Pigs: Baby Guinea pigs are called pups. They are born with instant cuteness, as they are fully furred and have open eyes. They appear to be perfect miniature versions of the adults! They'll even begin to eat some solid food just a few days after birth. Don't let this fool you, however. They still need their mother's milk for at least four weeks after birth.

Determining the sex of the pups can be a challenge, due to the immaturity of their genitalia, but this gets easier with practice. The Y shape beneath the anus is similar for both sexes, but the males have a small dot in the middle. You'll have to separate the sexes right after weaning, as both the males and females can begin the reproduction process at about one month of age! You should allow males to mature to two to three months old, and females to mature to at least five months old, before breeding them.

THERAPY PETS

Raising baby piggies can be an awesome adventure, but it also requires a lot of work. An activity that does not involve as much cleanup and fuss is pet therapy work. Therapy work is not often associated with Guinea pigs, but therapy pets can come in just about any size or species.

You don't necessarily have to join a therapy group to do therapy work with your pet. Although these groups can provide valuable instruction and support, you can "go it alone" if you feel comfortable and confident doing it this way. You can contact nursing homes and other facilities on your own to see who might be interested in receiving visits from your furry friend.

Guinea pigs that enjoy being handled can make great therapy pets.

If your Guinea pig has a calm demeanor and genuinely loves human attention, he may have what it takes to bring cheer to those who need it. A therapy pet can provide companionship and affection to the elderly, the infirm, hospitalized children, or inmates, depending on the type of therapy program you and your Guinea pig join. There are a few things to consider, however, when using such a small animal as a therapy pet.

Guinea pigs can be easily injured if they're handled improperly. An elderly person or a child might handle the animal too roughly, or accidentally drop it, so it may be best if you do the holding while the recipients of your goodwill do the petting. You need to exercise good judgment in deciding what types of interactions will be allowed for each person you encounter. It is your responsibility to protect your Guinea pig from harm at all times.

If you think you'd like to share your special pet with others, you can contact a therapy animal group in your area. The Delta Society Pet Partners Program provides a listing of therapy groups on its Web site, www.deltasociety.org.

TRAVELING

Guinea pigs are naturally nervous animals and can become easily stressed in new environments. Your piggy is as excited about traveling as most cats are about swimming. If you can avoid traveling with your little guy, he'll be much happier having a neighbor, friend, or pet sitter taking care of his needs while you're gone.

TAKING YOUR GUINEA PIG WITH YOU: There are occasions that may require an excursion with your pet, such as a trip to the vet's office, a change of residence, or travel to a show. In these cases, you should transport your Guinea pig in a pet carrier to keep him safe. Your Guinea pig will feel much more comfortable in his carrier if he is already accustomed to it. Use the carrier to hold your pet every time you clean his cage, and give him a

ROAD RULES

- Don't require your Guinea pig to travel unless it is absolutely necessary.
- If possible, use a seat belt to secure your pet's carrier in the vehicle.
- Never leave your pet in the car unattended, as he is vulnerable to theft and extreme temperatures.
- For longer road trips, be sure to offer your Guinea pig food and water.
- A towel placed over the carrier (leave the door uncovered for ventilation) can help minimize the stress for your pet.

A small pet carrier can help keep your Guinea pig safe when you travel.

piece of carrot to keep him busy. He'll soon learn that the carrier is a temporary but pleasant place to be.

When transporting your Guinea pig by car, secure your pet's carrier with a seat belt if possible. You can keep your buddy calm by putting a towel over his carrier, but make sure the door is uncovered for ventilation. Remember: never leave your pet in the car unattended, as this can expose him to theft or extreme temperatures!

If you need to travel by plane, you should use an airline that will allow your Guinea pig to accompany you in the cabin. Your pet's sensitivity to heat and cold means that traveling in the cargo hold without climate control could be deadly. Check with the airline to find out exactly what is required for your Guinea pig to travel by air.

Leaving Your Guinea Pig at Home: One of the reasons Guinea pigs make such nice pets is that it's easy to find someone to care for them when you're gone! They don't need to be let outside to do their business, they don't need to be taken for walks, and they won't soil the house or destroy the furniture while you're away. Who could resist an opportunity to take care of such a lovely critter?

You may be able to find a neighbor, friend, or relative who can come by once a day to take care of feeding and providing water for your little friend, especially for those short weekend getaways. For longer absences, you may want to hire a professional pet sitter, as she will be able to take care of many other house-care responsibilities. Bringing in the mail and newspapers, turning lights on and off to deter thieves, and cleaning out your piggy's cage might be more than you want to impose on a friendship.

Interview potential pet sitters carefully, as you will be entrusting both your pet and your home to them. Pet sitting organizations, such as the National Association of Professional Pet Sitters (www.petsitters.org) and Pet Sitters International (www.petsit.com), maintain membership lists on their Web sites. You might also get good referrals from acquaintances.

CARING FOR YOUR SENIOR GUINEA PIG

Guinea pigs don't show their age as obviously as some other species, which is why it is difficult to tell how old they are just by looking at them. There are some physical conditions, like fatty eye or impaction (see Common Health Conditions in

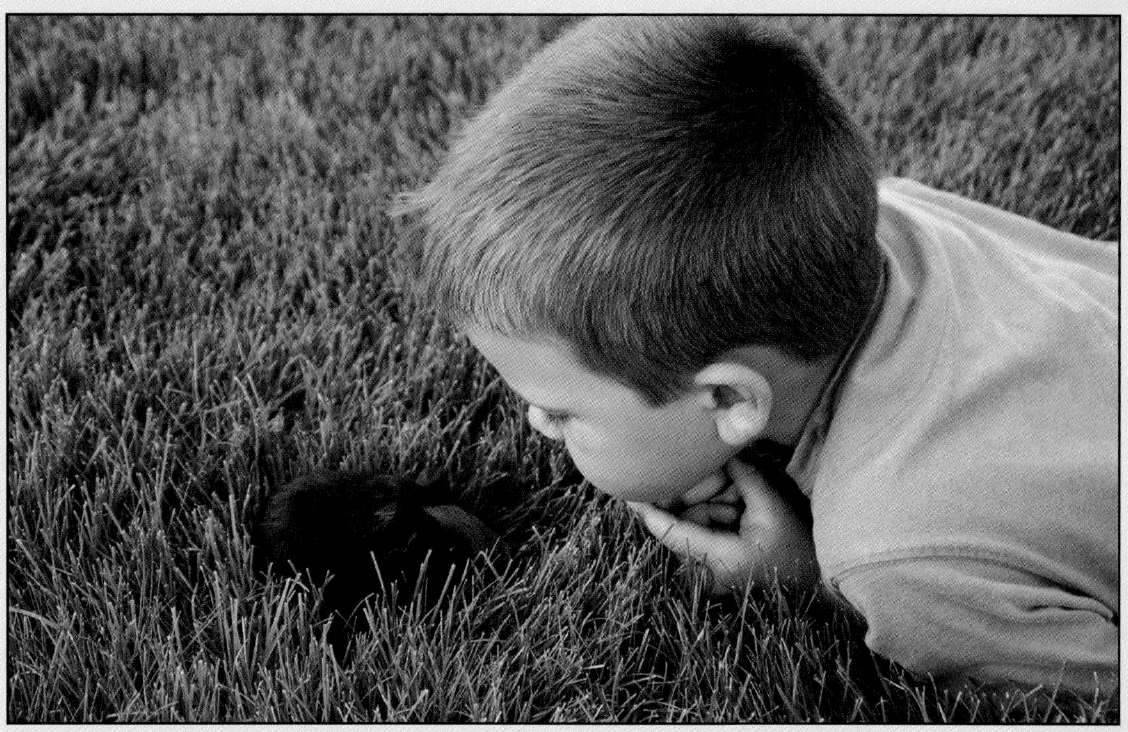

As your pet ages, he'll still enjoy doing things he did when he was younger, such as playing outside.

Chapter 6), that indicate that a Guinea pig is getting on in years. But Guinea pigs never really lose their youthful spirit.

As long as your pet continues to receive a healthful diet and get adequate exercise, he'll be in good shape throughout his life. Hopefully, he'll live out his entire life span of five to seven years and die a natural death of old age.

EUTHANASIA

As ideal as it sounds to allow nature to take its course, a natural death isn't always a pretty thing. If your aged Guinea pig is suffering prolonged pain or cannot be persuaded to eat, it is much kinder to relieve his suffering by assisting his transition from this life. This can be done with euthanasia, an intravenous injection of medications that will put your pet to sleep and suppress his bodily functions until his heart slowly stops.

Euthanasia is a very quiet, peaceful death. It is the kind of passing that is not only easy on your pet, it is easy on you as well. It may seem like

Photos of your Guinea pig in happier times can help to ease the pain of his passing.

a difficult decision to make, but it can be even more excruciating to watch a beloved pet suffer. Your veterinarian can help you determine if euthanasia is the best option for your pet.

SAYING GOOD-BYE

It's never easy to say good-bye, even if you try to mentally prepare for it. It doesn't seem fair that most animals do not live as long as we do, but that is a sad fact of life. The best thing we can do is find a way to cope with it.

Your Guinea pig means a lot to you and has become an important part of your life, so when it is his time to pass, remember the good times you had with him instead of focusing on your loss. You can memorialize your pet in a number of ways so that you will have something to keep as a reminder of the time you shared together. Construct a photo collage you can hang on the wall, make a garden stone, or plant a tree or bush in your pet's memory.

How you handle your pet's remains can also help provide some closure. If you decide to bury your pet on your own property, check into local ordinances first, to make sure this is allowed. You can construct your own grave marker, or make this a family project so all family members have a chance to add their personal touch. Your veterinarian can offer other alternatives, such as having your pet's remains interred in a pet cemetery or having your pet's

FAST FACT

Euthanasia is a term that means "good death," and it definitely lives up to this name.

ashes put in an urn. Contrary to popular belief, burial plans are appropriate for any animal species, not just cats and dogs.

A loss is a loss, regardless of the type of pet that passes on, but healing can be found in many different, positive ways. You can make a donation to an animal shelter in your pet's name or volunteer your time and experience to care for unwanted, homeless Guinea pigs. In any case, it doesn't help to dwell on your loss, so keep busy and plan activities that will give you something to look forward to.

Sometimes, finding a new cavy friend is just what the doctor ordered. A new Guinea pig cannot replace the one you lost, but he will certainly bring back a few smiles. If you feel ready to make a commitment to a new piggy relationship, your new friend can help replace your grief with the promise of more excitement and fun!

❧❧❧

There should be fun in everything you do with your Guinea pig, from playing with him to cleaning up after him. Then, when it's time to say good-bye, you'll realize how much richer you are for having experienced the companionship of a Guinea pig. Love has no size, even when it comes in a small package.

Organizations to Contact

American Animal Hospital Association
P.O. Box 150899
Denver, CO 80215-0899
Phone: 303-986-2800
Fax: 800-252-2242
Email: info@aahanet.org
Web site: www.aahanet.org

American Cavy Breeders Association (ACBA)
28 Southdowns Dr.
Kokomo, IN 46902
Phone: 309-664-7500
Fax: 309-664-0941
Email: JJHYorkie@aol.com
Web site: www.acbaonline.com

American Holistic Veterinary Medical Association (AHVMA)
2218 Old Emmorton Road
Bel Air, MD 21015
Phone: 410-569-0795
Fax: 410-569-2346
Email: office@ahvma.org
Web site: www.ahvma.org

American Rabbit Breeders Association (ARBA)
8 Westport Court
Bloomington, IL 61702
Phone: 309-664-7500
Fax: 309-664-0941
Email: info@arba.net
Web site: www.arba.net

Association of Exotic Mammal Veterinarians (AEMV)
P.O. Box 396
Weare, NH 03281-0396
Phone: unlisted
Fax: 478-757-1315
Email: info@aemv.org
Web site: www.aemv.org

British Cavy Council
Secretary and Treasurer
Duncton Place
3 Fir Tree Close
Sudbrooke, Lincoln
LN2 2YG
United Kingdom
Email: secretary@
britishcavycouncil.org.uk
Web site:
http://britishcavycouncil.org.uk

Delta Society
875 124th Avenue NE, Suite 101
Bellevue, WA 98005
Phone: 425-226-7357
Fax: 425-679-5539

Email: info@deltasociety.org
Web site: www.deltasociety.org

National Association of Professional Pet Sitters (NAPPS)
17000 Commerce Parkway, Suite C
Mt. Laurel, NJ 08054
Phone: 856-439-0324
Fax: 856-439-0525
Email: napps@ahint.com
Web site: www.petsitters.org

National 4-H Headquarters
U.S. Department of Agriculture
1400 Independence Avenue, SW, Stop 2225
Washington, DC 20250-2225
Phone: 202-720-2908
Fax: 202-720-9366
Email: 4hhq@csrees.usda.gov
Web site: www.national4-hheadquarters.gov

Pet Sitters International (PSI)
201 East King Street
King, NC 27021-9161
Phone: 336-983-9222
Fax: 336-983-9222
Web site: www.petsit.com

Rare Varieties Cavy Club
Secretary / Treasurer
15 Blackthorn Close
Uppingham, Rutland
LE15 9BG
United Kingdom
Phone: 01572-823479
Email: jayne@jacrick.fsnet.co.uk
Web site: http://www.rvcc.co.uk

Further Reading

Gurney, Peter. *Proper Care of Guinea Pigs*. Neptune City, N.J.: T.F.H. Publications, Inc., 1999.

Orr, Joan, and Teresa Lewin. *Getting Started: Clicking with Your Rabbit*. Waltham, Mass.: Sunshine Books, Inc., 2006.

Parker Guidry, Virginia. *Guinea Pigs: Practical Advice to Caring for Your Guinea Pig*. Irvine, Calif.: Bowtie Press, 2004.

Standard of Perfection. Bloomington, Ill.: American Rabbit Breeders Association, Inc., 2006.

Vanderlip, Sharon, DVM. *The Guinea Pig Handbook*. Hauppauge, N.Y.: Barron's Educational Series, 2003.

Internet Resources

www.guineapiglynx.info

A great online medical care guide for Guinea pig owners.

www.cavyspirit.com

Lots of great information on this Guinea pig education, rescue, and adoption Web site.

www.gpdd.org

The *Guinea Pigs Daily Digest* is an e-mail newsletter with news about the Guinea pig world. It's fun and free!

www.guineapigs.org

The Guinea Pigs Rescue Organization's site provides a list of rescues that specialize in Guinea pigs, organized by country and state.

www.petfinder.com

Provides listings of adoptable Guinea pigs from shelters across the country.

Index

Abyssinian (breed), 30–31
Abyssinian Satin (breed), 31
adoption. *See* ownership
agouti (color), 27
allergies, 18, 26
American Animal Hospital Association (AAHA), 75
American (breed), 31
American Cavy Breeders Association (ACBA), 35
See also American Rabbit Breeders Association (ARBA)
American Holistic Veterinary Medical Association (AHVMA), 76
American Rabbit and Cavy Breeders Association. *See* American Rabbit Breeders Association (ARBA)
American Rabbit Breeders Association (ARBA), 25, 34, 35–36, 94
American Satin (breed), 31
Association of Exotic Mammal Veterinarians (AEMV), 75

bathing. *See* grooming
bedding, 50–51
See also supplies
breeders and breeding, 39–40, 95–97
breeds, 30–35
See also Guinea pigs
brindle (color), 27
British Cavy Council (BCC), 34, 35, 36
brushing. *See* grooming

cages, 47–48
See also supplies
cataracts, 83
See also health
"cavy." *See* Guinea pigs
cecotropes, 64–65, 84
See also diet
clicker training. *See* training
coat. *See* hair
colors, Guinea pig, 27–30, 34
See also physical characteristics
commercial feed, 60–61
See also diet
communication. *See* vocalizations
constipation, 84
See also health
coprophagy, 64–65
See also diet
Coronet (breed), 31–32

Dalmatian (color), 27, 34
death, 101–103
Delta Society Pet Partners Program, 99
See also therapy pets
diarrhea, 83–84
See also health
diet, 18, 60–65, 83
and obesity, 80–81
Dutch (color), 27

ear infections, 83
See also health

Numbers in ***bold italics*** refer to captions.

Elizabeth I (Queen), 25
euthanasia, 101–102
exercise, 60–61, 65
    and playtime, 88–90

fatty eye, 83
    See also health
fleas, 79
    See also parasites
fungal infections, 82–83
    See also health

gender differences, 43–45
grooming, 52–53, 65–70
    See also ownership
Guinea pigs
    breeds of, 30–35
    and children, 18–20, 56–57
    colors of, 27–30, 34
    and death, 101–103
    and diet, 18, 60–64
    as food, 23–24
    and gender differences, 43–45
    handling of, 15, 18, 39, 42, 54–56, 98
    and health issues, 74–87, 96
    as herd animals, 16–18
    and history, 10–11, 23–25, 26
    and home environments, 21–22, 46–51, 53–54
    life span of, 13, 16, 101
    organizations for, 25, 35–36
    and other pets, 20–21, 57–58
    physical characteristics, 12–15, 25–30, 33, 34, 42–43, 52, 71, 72, 81
    as pups, 97
    and scientific experiments, 26
    as seniors, 100–101
    and showing, 93–95
    and temperament, 15–19, 41–42, 45
    as therapy pets, 97–99
    and traveling, 99–100
    and vocalizations, 9, 11, 43
    See also ownership
Guyana, 10

hair, 13–14, 25–26
    colors, 27–30, 34
    and grooming, 52–53, 65–69
    See also physical characteristics
hay. *See* diet
health
    checks, 70–72
    issues, 74–87, 96
heat prostration, 80
    See also health
Himalayan (color), 28, 30
hutches, outdoor, 48–49

impaction, 84
    See also health
injuries, 84–86
    See also health

lice, 77
    See also parasites
litter box training, 48, 53, 72–73
    See also training

malocclusion, 81
    See also health
marked (color), 28
mites, 78
    See also parasites

nail trimming, 69–70

See also grooming
National Association of Professional Pet Sitters, 100
National Cavy Club (NCC), 36
See also British Cavy Council (BCC)
National Pet Stock Association, 25
nest boxes, 49–50
See also supplies
neutering, 86–87
New Guinea, 10
nutrition. *See* diet

obesity, 80–81
ownership, 9–10, 59–60
children and Guinea pigs, 18–20, 56–57
choosing a veterinarian, 75–76
choosing your Guinea pig, 37–45
and feeding, 18, 60–65, 80–81, 83
and grooming, 52–53, 65–70
and health checks, 70–72
and home environments, 21–22, 46–51, 53–54
and multiple pigs, 16–17, 44–45
neutering and spaying, 86–87
and rules, 56–58
and supplies, 16, 40, 50–53
and training, 48, 53, 72–73, 91–93
See also Guinea pigs

parasites, 77–79
See also health
personality. *See* temperament
Peru, 24–25
Peruvian (breed), 32
Peruvian Satin (breed), 32
pet carriers, 53, 99–100
See also supplies
Pet Sitters International, 100
physical characteristics
and choosing a Guinea pig, 42–43
color, 27–30, 34
glossary, 33
hair, 13–14, 25–30
head, 12–13
legs and feet, 14–15
size and weight, 13
teeth, 12–13, 52, 71, 72, 81
See also Guinea pigs
playtime, 88–90
See also exercise
popcorning, 45
pups, 97

Rare Varieties Cavy Club, 34
respiratory infections, 81–82
See also health
roan (color), 28, 34
roughage, 63–64
See also diet

Satin (color), 30
scurvy, 79–80
See also health
self (color), 28
senior Guinea pigs, 100–101
showing, 93–95
and breeding, 95–97
See also American Rabbit Breeders Association (ARBA)
Silkie (breed), 32–33
Silkie Satin (breed), 33
size and weight, 13
See also physical characteristics
solid (color), 28–29
spaying, 86–87

supplies, 16, 40, 50–53
    See also ownership

Teddy (breed), 33
Teddy Satin (breed), 34
teeth, 12–13, 52, 71, 72, 81
    See also physical characteristics
temperament, 15–19, 41–42, 45
Texel (breed), 34
therapy pets, 97–99
tortoiseshell and white (color), 30
tortoiseshell (color), 29–30
training, 91–93
    litter box, 48, 53, 72–73
    See also ownership
traveling, 99–100

vegetation, 61–63
    See also diet
veterinarians, 75–77
    See also health
vocalizations, 9, 11, 43

White Crested (breed), 34
worms, 78
    See also parasites

Contributors

Janice Biniok has written numerous articles and several books on companion animals. She has an English degree from the University of Wisconsin–Milwaukee and is a member of the Dog Writers Association of America, Inc. Janice lives on a small farm in Waukesha, Wisconsin, with her husband, two sons, and several four-legged members of the family. Her other books in the Our Best Friends series include *The Poodle*, *Rabbits*, and *The Yorkshire Terrier*.

Senior Consulting Editor **Gary Korsgaard, DVM,** has had a long and distinguished career in veterinary medicine. After graduating from The Ohio State University's College of Veterinary Medicine in 1963, he spent two years as a captain in the Veterinary Corps of the U.S. Army. During that time he attended the Walter Reed Army Institute of Research and became Chief of the Veterinary Division for the Sixth Army Medical Laboratory at the Presidio, San Francisco.

In 1968 Dr. Korsgaard founded the Monte Vista Veterinary Hospital in Concord, California, where he practiced for 32 years as a small animal veterinarian. He is a past president of the Contra Costa Veterinary Association, and was one of the founding members of the Contra Costa Veterinary Emergency Clinic, serving as president and board member of that hospital for nearly 30 years.

Dr. Korsgaard retired in 2000, and currently enjoys golf, hiking, international travel, and spending time with his wife Susan and their three children and four grandchildren.